Can you
keep a
secret?

Can you keep a secret?

MY LIFE AS
A SUBMISSIVE

Katie Collins
with Robert Carry

EBURY
PRESS

1 3 5 7 9 10 8 6 4 2

Published in 2012 by Ebury Press, an imprint of Ebury Publishing
A Random House Group company
First published in ebook by Y Books, Ireland in 2012

The Ra
Stewardship Council (FSC®), the leading international forest
certification organisation. Our books carrying the FSC label are
printed on FSC® certified paper. FSC is the only forest
certification scheme endorsed by the leading environmental
organisations, including Greenpeace. Our paper procurement
policy can be found at www.randomhouse.co.uk/environment

MIX
Paper from
responsible sources
FSC® C016897

Printed and bound by CPI Group (UK) Ltd, Croydon, CR0 4YY

ISBN 9780091951580

To buy books by your favourite authors and register for offers visit
www.randomhouse.co.uk

Dedicated to my ever-supportive mam.

DISCLAIMER

Names, dates, locations, occupations and other distinguishing details have been changed to protect the identities of the people in this book.

Katie Collins is a pseudonym.

Prologue

I was terrified. The adrenaline was making my hands shake. What the fuck was I doing? Was this what I wanted? Looking around the room, I wondered what had happened to me. I mean, this wasn't normal.

A brunette dressed in a skin-tight rubber dress and a pair of painfully high black heels was leading a man around the room on his knees by a leash. He was wearing a full, black, patent-leather, silver-studded gimp outfit. His mistress had a look of absolute contempt on her face. I was in over my head.

Just two parts of the brunette's 'pet' were visible. His eyes were left uncovered by the zip-on mask, and they darted around wildly as he snorted and grunted to draw breath through two tiny nostril holes. His erect cock was the other part of his anatomy that was on view to the room; it jutted from an opening in the

1

crotch of his outfit. I couldn't believe what I was seeing. I wasn't sure if I should gag, run or laugh.

Then there were the others. Every one of the thirty-strong crowd crammed inside the dimly-lit room was dressed in some manner of fetish gear. But some had decided to go further than others. Most of the girls wore thigh-high boots and corsets, while many of the men were decked out in leather trousers, black string vests and black eye make-up. Others, however, had gone the whole hog and were clad head-to-toe in leather and rubber.

At twenty-one I was the youngest girl in the room. To make things worse, everyone else seemed like they knew each other. Apart from Angelina, who was holding the end of a dog leash she had attached to the collar around my neck, I didn't know anyone. I looked at her for reassurance, but she had slipped into character as soon as the door closed shut behind us. My fun, cheerful friend was gone. In her place was a pitiless, stern dominatrix more likely to strap me to a wall and whip me raw than put a comforting arm around me. I took a deep breath and looked at the floor.

I felt like sprinting from the room for fear of being

kidnapped and detained as a pet gimp by these people. Even if things went well, there was a lot of pain coming my way. But something was making me stay. There was something bigger hiding behind the fear and the promise of the abuse and pain to come.

Although still young, I knew enough about my sexuality to recognise that I was a submissive. Ever since my earliest sexual experiences, I had always enjoyed the powerlessness of being with someone who could take control. I liked being reduced to a sexual plaything. I aimed to please. But lately, I had found myself daydreaming about what it would be like to go further. I wanted to test myself; to see how far beyond my comfort zone I was capable of going in my desire to please someone else. I wanted to feel pain. I wanted to be a victim. Well, this was where it all led.

I lifted my chin, took another giant gulp from my drink and steeled myself as best I could. Looking around for reassurance, I noticed a table of nibbles in one corner of the room. That had to be good. Nobody puts on nibbles and drinks for someone they're about to kidnap and press into a life of sexual servitude. But the selection of nuts and triangle-cut ham sandwiches were about the only things in the room from which I could draw comfort. The venue itself was a converted stable attached to an old Victorian property off one of Dublin city centre's historic streets. Coarse, white-washed walls, gnarled oak beams, black flagstone floors – the event organisers had chosen well. They had amplified the stable's vague air of menace by kitting it out with a slightly terrifying array of fetish gear. They were going for the dungeon look – and they had hit the mark.

A six-foot-high, black, wooden X leaned against one wall. It had studded ankle and wrist straps nailed into each corner. A huge selection of dildos, whips, masks and chains dangled from wall hooks, and there were even more displayed on tables around the room. The room's centrepiece was a black, leather-clad table, the top of which had been cut roughly into the shape of a person. It too had leather cuffs attached.

I noticed the resident dominatrix having a conversation with a second submissive – a slightly portly gentleman in rubber shorts, with a bright-red ball gag in his mouth. His lips flapped and slobbered as he struggled to communicate past a bright red ball

4

gag. Then, all of a sudden, his mistress grabbed him by the throat and dragged him across the room towards the big wooden X. As she strapped him to the frame, the dominatrix unleashed a torrent of abuse at the guy. Next she picked up a cat-o'-nine-tails whip and set about lashing the arse off him.

This violent turn of events completely changed the atmosphere in the room. Until then, people had been chatting, sneaking glances at each other and generally attempting, as best they could, to avoid looking ridiculous in their outlandish outfits. But after the dominatrix landed that first crack on her submissive's backside, she had everyone's rapt attention.

It was shocking to see this type of thing for real, but it made for compelling viewing. It certainly beat a night in front of the telly. I felt lucky. I was getting the inside track on something people rarely get to see.

The guy's reddening face twisted and contorted with each whip and he strained against his binds. His dominatrix, however, was unconcerned by his struggle. She continued whipping with ever-increasing force. Despite the fact that the man looked like he was about to have a stroke, there was no shortage of volunteers willing to hand themselves up for punishment. While most of the crowd was moving in for a closer look, others were forming queue. When ball-gag man was finally liberated, nodding mute thanks at his tormentor, another victim stepped eagerly into his place. And so it went.

My turn came when the brunette mistress walked up to Angelina and asked if she could borrow me. 'She's all yours,' said Angelina, handing over my leash.

I was being passed around like they owned me, but rather than being horrified by the idea, I was turned on by it. The mistress yanked on my chain and led me over to the leather table in the centre of the room. My heart pounded as I noticed the rest of the room turning their attention to me. A heavily tattooed guy dressed in leather trousers and little else took a black-leather, tasselled whip from the wall and walked towards us. He looked about thirty and had a shaved head and a cut upper body. He didn't look like the sort of guy who spent his time flexing in gym mirrors – he had a ripped, sinewy frame men only get from hard physical work. He looked like he could punch holes through walls.

'Get onto the fucking table, you little bitch,' snapped the mistress.

Her long, dark hair fell down around a beautiful, if heavily made-up face. But her crimson lips were twisted into a wicked sneer. Maybe she didn't like me looking at her man. My heart raced and my palms sweated as I climbed onto the table.

I lay face down and closed my eyes. I felt ill with terror and excitement as the mistress and her man fastened the cuffs tightly around my ankles and wrists. I could hear their metal rings jangling slightly as my hands shook. One second I felt I was in over my head, the next I was revelling in the exhilaration of submisssion.

Fixed to the table with a circle of spectators jostling for a better look, I felt a sudden crack across my backside as the whip came down. It stung sharply, causing me to catch my breath. If I thought he was going to take it easy on me because I was new, I was mistaken. But as the shock of the first blow faded, it was replaced by a warm, pleasant sensation that spread from where he hit me up through my stomach and out to my bound limbs. It was painful, but I wasn't experiencing the pain in the way you would when you stub your toe or step on a plug. In the fog of adrenaline and alcohol, a pleasurable undertone was coming through in ever stronger waves. It was just as well. He hitched up my skirt so he could whip bare skin, and the blows kept coming. I bit down. I endured.

While I was being whipped, his partner took me by the hair and tilted my head back. She slapped me gently on the face, before smiling and letting my head drop back on the table. The drinks I'd hurriedly put away in a desperate attempt to calm my tattered nerves were taking effect, and the room became a blur of whipping, slapping and insults.

At one point, the guy had removed my underwear and was roughly pushing two fingers inside me. The dominatrix meanwhile, who had taken the whip from him, was lashing me unmercifully while spitting insults through those bright-red lips, telling me what a filthy whore I was. But rather than hurting me, all the abuse and the insults and the whipping were rolling over me in waves of spine-jangling pleasure. I looked to my right; another guy in a gimp suit was taking his turn on the X-frame. Strapped in place, his head lolling with the blows of the whip, he stared at me with vacant, glassy eyes. I remember thinking, *Have I crossed the line? How can I ever go back to a normal life after this?* But if there is a line, I had probably crossed it long before that night.

I didn't wake up one morning and decide to get involved in such an extreme scene. In fact, right from my first tentative steps as a curious fourteen-year-old into what was then a strange new world, my sex life had always been a little extreme. But by the time I was being strapped to that table, my search for new sexual experiences, coupled with a ferocious sexual appetite, had sent my sex life into the stratosphere.

Before I was even eighteen I began meeting men in sex-related internet chatrooms and sleeping with any I found attractive. Dozens of them. Three in one day, sometimes. I had got involved in threesomes, foursomes and moresomes, before diving headlong into Ireland's swinging scene. I took part in gangbangs, had sex with women in front of dozens of men and fucked on webcam while hundreds watched open-mouthed. I handed my body over to men I didn't know, and I enthusiastically embraced the use of ropes, cuffs, blindfolds and all manner of accessories.

By the time I reached twenty-one I was the youngest, filthiest and most popular girl in Dublin's underground sex scene and I milked it for all it was worth. I had the sex life millions secretly fantasise about but don't have the nerve to make a reality. This is my story.

Chapter One

There was nothing in my early years to suggest the direction my life would go in. I grew up at the end of a quiet road in a Dublin suburb. Our house was at the bottom of the street and my nana's house was nearby. I was the baby of the family, with one older sister.

Unusually for Dublin, we were not brought up Catholic. My mother drifted away from the church when I was barely out of nappies. But rather than avoid religion altogether, she had a habit of drifting from one faith to another – and of taking the whole family with her.

I have memories of being dragged in and out of various houses of prayer around the city and of having interchangeable religious types regularly dropping by our house. My da was never religious. He had good reason to be sceptical of the idea of a beatific God smiling down on us. When he was twelve, his grandfather and father both dropped dead within nine days of each other. His grandmother had died giving birth to his mother, and because his mother was an only child, the deaths of his grandfather and father meant his family was practically wiped out in one go. It was just him and his mother, and she took to drink.

My da was never into running down anyone else's beliefs; he was polite enough to go to church for weddings and christenings. He was friendly towards the people my mother brought to our house, but he tended to suddenly think of something he had to go and do whenever they turned up.

The one big downside to my mother's à-la-carte approach to religion was that while all the other kids in my school prepared for the cash windfall that comes with their First Holy Communion, I would have to sit it out. I was bitterly disappointed, and I grew resentful of my mother's religious choices.

It's not unusual for an Irish person to have family members who battle the demon drink, and my grandmother and both my parents were alcoholics. Of the three, alcoholism suited my ma best. She managed to work, drive and maintain a household whilst pissed on her daily bottle of vodka. In addition to my da having issues with drink, he also had a long-standing gambling problem, although I wasn't aware of it when I was a kid. My parents split when I was eight and my da initially refused to move out of the family home. In the end, my ma packed up my sister and me and moved into another house, about ten minutes away.

My father was in and out of work for most of my early life. He worked as a lorry driver for a while, driving around Ireland in a big truck. He would occasionally pack my sister and me into the cab and bring us with him down the country for the day. There were the two big seats in the front of his truck, and a third little one in the centre. I was the smallest so I sat in the middle. Da was a binman for a time, and he also worked in Dublin Airport, but there were big gaps in his employment history.

Despite the issues that had led to my parents' split, there wasn't a major fall out and my da continued to be part of my life. I used to see him every weekend, and we would go to the park or the cinema, or maybe just for a walk. Sometimes he didn't show and although I don't recall it myself, my ma told me that he was still an active alcoholic at that stage. She also told me that he would occasionally turn up drunk. However, he had given up alcohol by the time I was old enough to notice so I have no real memory of him being anything other than the sober man he is now.

I was equally oblivious to my mother's drink problem. She managed it so well that I didn't notice she was putting away a bottle of vodka a day. It wasn't that she went out of her way to hide it – she would occasionally even ask me to pour her drinks – but I didn't think anything of it and it never registered as an issue. Strangely, she seemed to function better while pissed. She never once had an accident in all her years of driving around hammered but she's had several bumps and scrapes since giving up. She was as fully functional as functioning alcoholics come.

The guilt of living in a house right next to the school his kids had to trek to each morning obviously started to get to my da, and when I was about twelve, he decided to move out and let us have the house. The visits continued as always and we maintained a good relationship with him.

A psychologist would no doubt point to a broken family, a missing father and a resultant craving for male attention as triggers for my somewhat extreme behaviour later on. But I don't think my sexual preferences started with daddy issues. I don't think that my da moving out when I was little prompted me to develop a fixation with male attention. In reality I was probably too young to feel the full impact of the break-up. My older sister, however, might not have been. She became pregnant at sixteen. She had a son and quickly became pregnant again with her second child. My ma didn't have a degree in psychology but she always maintained that not having my da around was the key driver behind my sister's problems.

I was ten when my sister had her first child and eleven when she had her second. Having the kids around was no different to having younger siblings in the house. I loved looking after them. This worked out well because my sister was the sociable, gregarious type and she loved going out. My ma wasn't the happiest about the situation but she was supportive of my sister. She was proud of her for being pro-life when many in her shoes would have chosen to take the boat to England for an abortion.

Primary school was a happy place for me. It was a small school and everyone knew everyone. I had plenty of friends, but that all changed when I went to secondary school. The school was huge, impersonal and I knew nobody. The transition coincided with puberty; it was like they timed it deliberately to make life as difficult as possible. There were hoards of skinny, giggling girls, with whom I didn't fit in. I suddenly realised that I had gone through primary school completely oblivious to the fact that I was an overweight tomboy. I had always worn tracksuits and hoodies, and I was rocked by the sudden realisation that I looked awful. I never got bullied but I didn't make any friends either. I became a loner.

My sister wasn't in a position to help. She was an outgoing girly girl and had started working as a hairdresser shortly after I started in secondary school. We got on well but we didn't have a lot in common, so we tended to spend very little time together. There were never jealousy issues but at that age we were poles apart.

I was alone – until a saviour of sorts turned up. People blame the internet for corrupting young people and, to be honest, I think they're right. I now believe that it's a bad idea to give unrestricted internet access to a teenage girl. To do so is akin to letting a mob of sexual predators loose in your spare room. I was an oblivious, innocent, socially awkward thirteen-year-old when we got our first, painfully slow, dial-up connection. There was practically no social activity in my life, so it was only a matter of time before I found my way into a chatroom.

I was a wall flower in the real world. I was so anonymous at school that I felt transparent. The net was different. The first time I logged into a chatroom, there was a queue of guys willing to chat with me. The attention was flattering, and within days of making this discovery I was spending as much time as I could online. I spent hours on Yahoo Chat, a site since shut down due to the fact that it fast became home to a nest of paedophiles. Even though my profile said I was thirteen, it tended to be grown men who attempted to strike up conversations. For my part, I wasn't particularly fussed about age. If a guy was interesting and fun to talk to, then age didn't seem relevant to me.

I chatted with plenty of guys from Ireland, but I preferred those from places like the UK or the US. I was still getting used to talking to members of the opposite sex and I found I was more comfortable chatting with men who were miles away. Either way, it was easier than the face-to-face version of human interaction.

Being bombarded with attention and compliments caused the feelings of self-consciousness that stalked me during school hours to quickly evaporate. The internet rapidly went from hobby to addiction and I began to spend every waking hour camped in front of the monitor, in the spare room.

Guys stated to request that I go on webcam so they could see me. Initially, I didn't think I could do it. I was still carrying some baby fat and I couldn't bear the idea of being rejected by my new online 'friends'. But I decided to investigate. I turned on my webcam when nobody was viewing so I could see how I would look on screen. All I could see was a pretty face looking back at me. It was a revelation. By manipulating camera angles and choosing what I wanted to show, I could do a lot to hide the weight problem I was still struggling with. There was further reassurance in the fact that I could click off the camera whenever I wanted to. I was in control.

Most other people who were brave or stupid enough to go on webcam with strangers in chatrooms hid their faces and protected their identity by angling their cameras downwards. I didn't think it was all that likely I would be spotted by anyone I knew in person, so I thought my chances of being recognised and getting in trouble were slim. Plus, my face was my best asset and I wasn't about to waste it. Once I made my onscreen debut, the number of guys hoping to talk to me exploded. Dozens fired me requests to view my cam, and I couldn't see the harm in letting them.

I quickly discovered that when a female logs into a chatroom and strikes up a conversation with a guy, even if she happens to be a thirteen-year-old girl, it's only a matter of time before the subject of sex comes up. It would normally be sneaked in among a volley of compliments, and because the topic cropped up so often I gradually grew more comfortable talking about it. I started digging around the net for porn and it wasn't long before my head was well and truly turned. A new, previously alien world opened up in front of me.

My growing interest in sex was going in an unusual direction. Everything was online – I didn't even know what it was like to kiss someone. I would later be happy to perform the most intimate acts with strangers while yet more strangers looked on, but back then the idea of doing anything in person seemed alien and slightly terrifying. Online flirting seemed mild by comparison – in the flesh you couldn't click a mouse and make the guy you're kissing disappear. So, when the guys who approached me online started suggesting I flash or strip on cam, it seemed like a natural, and relatively harmless progression. After months of being egged on, I took a deep breath and gave it a go.

Guys would ask me to lift up my top and play with my breasts, and I enjoyed the reaction I got when I did. I seemed to have so much control over them and how they felt. Another benefit was the warm, fuzzy feeling I got from a further spike in chat requests, compliments and positive attention.

Teasing men on the internet became the most enjoyable thing I did. They would tell me about how they were getting their cocks out when I started to play around on camera, but I was never interested in seeing them. I wasn't turned on by watching guys; I was turned on by them watching me. Yahoo Chat used to limit the number of people who can view a cam at any one time to ninety-nine, and I regularly hit the limit.

Looking back, it was straight-up grooming on their behalf but at the time I just didn't see it that way. I was there for what I got out of it and there didn't seem to be any downside. While most people would consider stripping on a webcam to be fairly advanced sexual behaviour, to me it seemed like a baby step compared to even holding a guy's hand. These men were sometimes thousands of miles away and I felt I had complete control over how and when anything happened. As far as I was concerned, this was all fantasy and bore little relation to the real world.

The only obvious negative was the amount of time I was spending online. It got to a point where I sat in front of the computer as soon as I got home from school, and would stay there until long after the rest of the family had turned in for the night. I would eventually stumble, bleary-eyed, into bed at five or six in the morning, before getting up for school a couple of hours later.

I already had little interest in school and having an alternative way to spend my time meant it quickly slipped further down my list of priorities. My ma left for work each morning before I had to leave for school, so going on the hop was never difficult. I was soon staying home more often than I was going in. I would sometimes break up the days I'd taken off by wandering around Dublin city centre, or by going to the cinema if I had the money, but most of the time I would just camp in front of the computer.

The chatroom pull-factor wasn't the only reason why I liked to bunk off school. Even in small doses secondary school was killing me. All the other girls seemed to be gorgeous and they all dressed in nice clothes. I was an anonymous fat girl in a fleece. It upset me terribly. I remember my ma asking me if everything was okay at school, and I said that I found it strange that I could be surrounded by so many people but yet still feel so alone.

It wasn't all the fault of the kids in my school – I alienated myself, too. Whenever I felt even slightly uncomfortable in the company of other people, I would clam up and say nothing. Even when I was sitting at home with my own mother, I would sometimes struggle and worry about what I should say. I couldn't understand how people could just happily chat bullshit with each other all day.

Eventually the net handed me a coping mechanism already adopted by troubled teenage girls the world over: self-harm. I stumbled onto sites that gave guidance on how to go about committing suicide and although that wasn't something I thought of resorting to, they also gave instruction on self-harm best practice. Don't go too deep. Use a razor blade rather than a knife. Keep it superficial. When you followed these guidelines, the cuts clear up in two weeks and leave practically nothing by way of scars. So one day I got a razor blade, went to my room and sat on my bed. I felt like shit and the theory was that physically harming myself was going to make me feel better. Hurting yourself to feel good sounds ridiculously counter-intuitive, but it worked.

I've lost count of the number times I've been asked about what I got out of self-harm, and I've always struggled to explain it. Some teenagers punch a pillow or a wall as a way of venting when they get angry. It gives them some temporary relief. I suppose cutting did the same for me. With no shortage of things to upset me, I found myself turning to self-harm a lot.

It got so bad that I used to spend my lunch break slicing my arms up with a razor blade, in a locked cubicle in the school toilets. When I was finished, I'd mop up the blood as best I could, pull my sleeves down and go back to class. The wounds healed fast, but I was cutting so often I always had to wear long sleeves to cover the fresh slash marks. In the end, that's what gave the game away to my parents.

I was sitting in a park with my da one Saturday when he asked why I was wearing long sleeves in the sun. I didn't have an answer and he demanded I show him my arms. I was horribly embarrassed. He looked gutted with worry. He did his best to find out why I was doing it, but I just couldn't find a way to explain it to him. He tried to reassure me by telling me that whatever was bothering me wouldn't last forever, but I just clammed up. He didn't understand what was happening to me and, as much as he wanted to, he couldn't give me a solution.

Things came to a head one day after I had a row with my ma. I was upset, so I ran into my room, grabbed a razor blade and cut hard into my arm. The blade wasn't as blunt as I thought and the cut just fell open, showing the fatty tissue underneath. It was bad: four inches long and half an inch wide. It wasn't painful, but the extent of the damage I had just done scared the shit out of me. So much so that my mother was instantly forgiven. I screamed for her to help me and she came running into the room.

My ma went from shouting at me for doing something so stupid over a non-event argument to asking if I was okay in all of five seconds. She worked as a home carer and had some medical training, so she knew how to treat the cut. She got one of her mattress-sized sanitary towels, wrapped it around my arm and held it up. She wanted to bring me to the hospital, but I refused to go. I couldn't face it. So she set up a pull-out bed right next to mine. I spent the night with my arm sticking out while my ma, lying on the pull-out, held it up. I remember saying at one stage during the night that my hand was getting cold, so she put a sock on it.

The next morning my mother looked at the cut – the edges were starting to curl in and she was adamant that she was taking me to the hospital. After a long wait we were finally brought in for treatment. I burned with embarrassment as they cleaned and stitched the cut. I managed to avoid most of the awkward questions, but my ma spent ages talking in hushed tones to concerned medical staff. My da came to the hospital and tried again to get through to me, this time just by asking me straight out what was wrong. I told him I didn't know. I felt like a dope. In the end, they decided to send me to a counsellor.

Chapter Two

I was to have hour-long counselling sessions every two weeks. My counsellor was a friendly, middle-aged woman with a kind face, who started by asking me about the previous couple of years. Surprisingly, I found it quite easy to open up to her. Eventually, after a string of visits and a verbatim account of my full fourteen years on the planet, she got around to asking me why I harmed myself. 'Out of frustration,' I said.

I asked her to imagine putting a potato in the microwave without cutting any holes in it – it would just explode. Cutting the skin relieves the pressure. She said it was a really interesting analogy, and a very smart thing to say.

Just talking about it all helped. Strangely, venting to a counsellor worked in the same way that cutting myself had. Instead of suffering under a general sense of foreboding that I couldn't attribute to anything in particular, talking things through helped me to identify more specifically the things that were bothering me. After a couple of months of therapy, my counsellor concluded that I was suffering from depression. It was decided that the next step was a referral to my GP – I was to be put on medication.

I was given a light anti-depressant called Lustral and, although I was sceptical, it helped immediately. I stopped feeling like crap for no reason. I still got pissed off when bad things happened, but if things were okay, I felt okay. The course of Lustral wasn't designed as a long-term solution. Instead, it was supposed to give my system a boost and get me on track before I reduced my dose or quit completely. In the meantime, my fortnightly chats with the counsellor continued.

Although I didn't feel comfortable enough to talk face-to-face about how I felt with anyone other than my counsellor, I sometimes broached the subject with my virtual friends. I found them easier to talk to because they didn't really know me. I felt I could say whatever I liked, without repercussions. Who cared what I said to them? At the click of a mouse they could be gone from my life forever.

The scars on my arms were beginning to heal and, when in my more positive frame of mind, I started to feel oddly proud of them. I rolled up my sleeves to display my array of scars when on the bus, almost hoping to get a reaction from people. I had gone through the pain of inflicting them, so I thought I might as well get some entertainment out of them.

There were a couple of slips but for the most part, I was able to put self-harm behind me. My ma, however, was still terrified I would do serious damage to myself again. I could see where she was coming from and I felt bad that she was so scared for me. She quit the drink around that time and, in the midst of a dogfight with alcoholism, it was the last thing she needed. She would sometimes come into my room in the middle of the night to check I was okay.

My browsing history didn't help. I used to look at Rotten.com, a stunningly morbid site populated with videos and pictures of car crashes, people being executed, deformed babies and everything else a happy, healthy individual shouldn't be looking at. I remember spotting a clip of a particularly nasty Iraqi beheading video, and I called my ma to take a look.

It showed an Asian guy who had been caught by Iraqi rebels. He screeched as the executioner sawed into the back of his neck. His screams continued until they hit his vocal chords, and then all he could do was make a gargling sound. People say that when your body suffers a major trauma like that you would be so full of adrenaline that you wouldn't feel a thing. No way. He could feel it all right. My ma was horrified, and, not surprisingly, she told me I shouldn't watch that type of thing. She said I was becoming desensitised, and she was right. I didn't feel anything beyond a detached curiosity.

My ma had another reason to worry. Back in those dark days of dial-up internet, being online was charged by the minute at the rate of a local call. The bills started to stack up and my mother became very keen to limit the amount of time I spent online. The financial argument didn't convince me, and I would sneak online whenever I could. It got to the point where she had a slide bolt and padlock fitted to the door of the spare bedroom so I couldn't get to the computer. It was infuriating. I often made arrangements to chat to a certain guy at a particular time, and being denied access to the computer left me seething with frustration. But even when I hadn't made an arrangement with someone I would still crave the chatrooms. I felt I was I was missing something when I wasn't plugged into them. It was an addiction. I couldn't get enough of it and everything else in my life was pushed to the side. I was a net junkie. Not only was I entirely incapable of giving up, I couldn't even contemplate the idea easing off a bit.

Happily, my ma usually relented to some degree and access would be restored. She knew I went into chatrooms so I'm sure she was curious about the things I spoke about, but vague answers kept my online social life separate from my real life. What I couldn't hide from my mother was that she was being billed for internet time when I was supposed to be at school. But there was even a way to get around that issue – I used one of the dozens of internet cafés dotted around Dublin city centre that charged tiny hourly rates.

At around fourteen, I got interested in piercing. I was coming to the end of a week-long stay in England with relatives and I had £50 spending money left over on my last day. I wanted to spend it on something before I left, and the idea of getting my eyebrow pierced popped into my head. I texted my ma to see if it was okay and when she said I could go ahead, I roped my uncle into bringing me to a studio.

The piercing was done with a needle but the pain was bearable. I was happy with the result. The downside came when, within hours of leaving the studio, my da found out and went ballistic. He spent that night calling around my family in England, trying to get me on the phone. He was furious that my ma had given me permission to do something like that without consulting him. He had become worried that he wouldn't have a full say in his children's upbringing post-separation and this, for him, was a perfect example. He was furious with me, too. He thought I'd done it to piss him off.

The problem with piercing is that it can get you hooked, and when I came home I wanted more. But annoyingly, I could barely hold onto the one I had.

When I turned up in school with my new facial ornament I was forced to take it out on the spot. I put it back in at weekends or when I had time off, but it was a constant battle to prevent it closing up. I decided my next piercing would be somewhere not vulnerable to inspection by the school authorities.

I started to pester my ma with the somewhat ambitious request that she take me to get my nipple pierced. I would have happily marched straight into a piercing studio alone, but I was still fourteen and I looked it. I needed an adult to take me. I strengthened my argument by pointing out that I would simply get a needle and do it myself if she didn't give me permission. Surely she would prefer me to get it done in a reputable studio rather than have me attempt a DIY job?

Surprisingly, she agreed. She felt that as a nipple piercing wouldn't be seen by anyone (she didn't know about the men who would be checking it out in batches of ninety-nine on webcam), it wasn't a big deal, certainly not as significant as the eyebrow piercing she had already agreed to. So the two of us went to a piercing shop and she signed the form to say I had parental consent to go ahead with the procedure. I had been talking about it like it was my God-given entitlement to have my nipple pierced but I was secretly stunned by what I was about to get away with.

When the day came, I started to feel like a fourteen-year-old probably should when she is about to face a needle that would skewer an intimate body part. Bizarrely, the idea of putting myself on display was even more terrifying than the needle. It was strange that I could happily whip my top off and play with my tits in front of dozens of men online, but doing it in person in front of one guy, even in a non-sexual scenario such as this one, was cripplingly scary. I was shaking with nervousness when I went into the studio. I was glad my ma was with me.

I thought lifting my top and pulling down my bra a little would be the extent of my exposure, but the stunningly unfriendly man explained that I had to be topless in order for him to get the symmetry right. I felt my cheeks flush as I took off my top. Why was I doing this to myself? My misery was amplified by the fact that there was a mirror directly opposite – I had to sit and look at myself topless in a room with a strange, grumpy man, and my mother in my peripheral vision. In a unique, needlessly unpleasant manner that was all his own, the piercer pushed my shoulders back to see how my breasts would sit. Next, he used a biro to mark out where he would make the incision.

The piercing itself was sickeningly painful, but the whole experience was upsetting. I pulled my top back on, feeling justifiably sorry for myself. I couldn't understand why the guy had been such a prick, but on reflection it must have been a tad unnerving for him too. Being a grown man in a room with a topless fourteen-year-old and her mother probably isn't fun.

But despite the pain and the awkwardness, there was one bright spot. The searing jolt of adrenaline I felt just before the piercing went through was nice, really nice. It made me want another one. With a signed waiver from my mother already in hand, I could go back whenever I wanted. Within two weeks I'd had the other nipple pierced. Happily, the arsehole that carried out the procedure first time wasn't around on my second visit. A far friendlier, far less terrifying female apprentice did the deed.

My real and online lives crossed paths for the first time when I was in an internet café on O'Connell Street when I should have been at school. The shop's computers were in two back-to-back rows so customers sat facing each other. I was in a Yahoo chatroom with the webcam turned on when a four-word instant message popped up on my screen.

'I can see you.'

I brushed it off until a second message came through.

'I'm at the front of the shop.'

My first reaction was to call the guards or beg the staff to help me. Then I recognised the nickname – it belonged to a guy I vaguely remembered chatting with previously. I got over the initial shock and I decided that I wasn't in any real danger. I was in the middle of a busy internet café in broad daylight. I might as well say hello.

I sent a message to say I would see him outside, paid up and walked nervously towards the exit. The guy was standing in the doorway looking at me when I approached. He was in his early twenties with lank, greasy hair and dark, troubled eyes. He also had the worst teeth I'd ever seen. They had a greenish layer of what looked like mould on them that almost made me gag. We chatted for a few minutes about nothing in particular. He did most of the talking while I waited for my chance to leave. It wasn't just his appearance that freaked me out. He was being outwardly nice, but he gave off a foul vibe. I finally managed to extricate myself by telling him I had to be home before my ma got back from work. He said no problem, but told me we should swap numbers first. I was intimidated and didn't want to turn the guy down flat, so I agreed. I didn't think to give him a fake number so I gave him my real one and then walked away with a shudder.

He texted me before I got home to ask when we could meet up again. I wasn't well equipped to handle the situation. I was shy and I didn't want to be rude, so I humoured him. Over the next few days, though, he became more and more insistent that we meet. With dozens of texts coming in daily, I eventually had to suck it up and tell him I wasn't interested. He didn't take it well.

He texted again, this time demanding to know where I lived. When I refused to tell him, he told me he would track me down and beat the shit out of me. I was terrified. For days I was too scared to leave my house. I felt couldn't tell anyone because it would mean explaining all the time I spent talking to strangers on the net and why I was in an internet café in the middle of the day instead of being at school. When I finally ventured out again, I avoided the café I met him in like the plague. Even so, for months I was looking over my shoulder whenever I was in the city.

But that bad experience didn't turn me off the idea of chatting with guys on the net; I just put it down to him being a bad apple. I saw little point in tarring every person in every chatroom with the one brush because of a scumbag who caught me off guard. Within weeks, I had found someone I wanted to meet.

I was fourteen years old. I was still a virgin. I hadn't as much as kissed a boy before and I was sitting in a car with a twenty-five-year-old off-duty garda I had met in an internet chatroom. He was barely recognisable as the person in the pictures he had sent me weeks earlier. It was the same guy all right, but the shots he emailed must have been at least five years old. He looked like a creep. His hairline was already losing its fight against an expanding forehead and what he had left of his hair was slicked back with far too much gel. He had small, rodent eyes that darted constantly from one thing to another.

I should have walked away the moment I got a look at him but instead, when he pulled in at the end of my road, I jumped straight into his car. We had been exchanging intimate, borderline-filthy texts for weeks, but once we were face-to-face the conversation was stilted and awkward. Beyond him asking if I knew somewhere quiet where he could park the car and me directing him to a suitably secluded spot, we said practically nothing to each other.

I suppose there was an inevitability about the whole thing. Chatting with random guys on the net had become my No. 1 hobby, so the time was bound to come when I would decide to go a step further. My age didn't prevent the offers from coming in – nearly everyone I spoke with asked me to meet them. I had, of course, heard the horror stories and I knew meeting a guy I only knew from the net was dangerous, but I was excited by the idea of turning some of the things I had talked about into reality.

John wasn't an obvious first choice. I had chatted with better-looking guys and he wasn't the most charming individual I had come across. What he did have going for him was his occupation. I was a naive kid and I thought the fact that he was a garda meant I would be safe with him. I thought of myself as being so grown up, but I didn't see the innate wrongness of a cop in his mid-twenties arranging to meet a fourteen -year-old in the hope of getting a blowjob.

John knew I was a virgin and that I wasn't interested in losing my virginity to him. I told him as much by text before we met and he had said it was fine, that he wasn't expecting me to. He said he still really wanted to meet me, on the understanding that we could do 'other stuff'. Although I wasn't old enough to legally consent to such a proposition, I decided to go ahead; a combination of boredom, curiosity and a somewhat rudimentary feeling of horniness combined to make me feel I wanted to.

So we arranged a time and a place and John came and picked me up. We had so far barely said two words to each other, but I got the impression that the lack of flowing conversation wouldn't get in the way of this 'other stuff' from happening. I had decided before he arrived that if he didn't have somewhere else in mind, I would suggest a car park close to one of Dublin's beaches. It was close to my home so it wouldn't take long to get there, and if he turned off his headlights we would be left alone. I noted another of its advantages as we pulled in – the absence of any street lighting meant much of this man's ugliness would be obscured by darkness.

I was nervous. I was tingling all over. One second I felt like opening the car door and sprinting away, and the next I felt like diving on him. The silence didn't help and I found myself hoping he would make the first move.

'Do you want to suck my dick?' John asked suddenly in what was more of a demand than a question.

He had been stern and quietly aggressive from the off, but his directness still caught me off guard. He was unbuttoning his jeans before he got the question out of his mouth and he had his hand on the back of my head before I could get out a reply. It didn't appear that I had any choice in the matter. It was a good thing I wanted to do it.

I had never given a blowjob before but a borderline addiction to porn, that developed shortly after the internet first arrived in our house, meant I at least knew what was expected of me. I leaned over to his side of the car, but as I put his cock into my mouth a thought occurred to me – we hadn't kissed yet. It wasn't that I really wanted to kiss him, but I would have liked to have had my first kiss before giving my first blowjob.

I bobbed up and down, taking as much of his dick as I could, but it didn't seem to be enough for John. He gripped the back of my head and started thrusting himself into my throat. He didn't stop when I started to gag and I was soon struggling to breathe. I reflexively ripped myself free in momentary panic. 'You fucker,' I spat with a watery-eyed glare.

I should have been scared, but I wasn't; I was just pissed off. The door wasn't locked and I knew the area, so I still felt I could jump out and run the few yards to the main road if I really needed to. To my mind things were still just about consensual, so I didn't feel he would turn nasty if I abruptly called a halt.

John watched me silently. He appeared to be assessing the situation, gauging my reaction to establish whether he had gone too far. He obviously decided that he hadn't because he suddenly cranked back my seat and jumped on top of me. 'I told you already – I'm not having sex,' I said with as much finality as I could manage. 'I'm not going to lose my virginity in a fucking car!'

He briefly tried to work my trousers off but the confined space made it difficult. He concluded that he wasn't going to get anywhere unless I agreed to help. 'Okay,' he grunted in a way that suggested he thought he was doing me a favour. 'You can go back to sucking me off.'

It was stunningly presumptuous of him, but his demand triggered something in me. I knew I shouldn't have, but I suddenly wanted to do what I was told. I was hoping he would be a bit gentler the second time but after a few seconds he was gripping the back of my head again. I had to fight to stop myself from gagging every time he rammed his dick into my throat, and by breathing through my nose I just about managed to take in enough air to stay conscious. John's body suddenly stiffened and he began grunting with each thrust. I was so inexperienced that I hadn't a clue what this meant and I was stunned when a jet of warm cum shot straight down my throat. I tried to pull away before the next spurt but he had a handful of my hair in each hand and was far too strong for me. I had no choice but to hold my breath and wait until he had finished empting himself into me.

I wrenched myself away as soon as he loosened his grip, gasping for breath while wiping my mouth on my sleeve. I had never come into contact with this salty stuff before and it felt and tasted vile. I glowered accusingly at John, but he just sat there looking pleased with himself. The thought of this man's cum in my stomach made me want to throw up. 'So will I drop you home then?' he said while buttoning himself up and smiling at me like nothing had happened.

I wanted to tell him what I thought of him, but I couldn't. I was shy. I was a kid, really, and I hated any type of confrontation. So I just nodded my head and he started up the car.

I noticed, as we drove silently towards where he had picked me up less than an hour earlier, that the glovebox had fallen open at some point. A set of pink fluffy handcuffs was visible inside.

'You use those for work?' I asked, trying desperately to take my mind off the queasiness I was feeling.

'You'd be surprised,' John said, with a dramatically raised eyebrow.

Within minutes, we were pulling up at the corner of my cul-de-sac.

'So do you want to meet up again?' he asked, as if we'd just had just enjoyed a polite dinner date.

I didn't have the nerve to turn him down flat to his face, so I said, 'Yeah, cool,' knowing I would never willingly see him again.

I stomped back into my house, ran upstairs and flopped onto my bed. Nobody had noticed I was gone. My heart was banging around in my chest at the thought of what had happened. I was fourteen and this had been my first time meeting a guy. Everyone I had chatted with online, John included, seemed so friendly and nice. Many had been a little preoccupied with sex, but I never thought any of them could behave like John had.

I knew I had been taken advantage of – John had made me do things I didn't want to do – but that isn't what strikes me most when I think about that night. What I find strangest is how I felt about it afterwards. I kept thinking that I should be horribly upset, but I wasn't. It had been a fucked-up, dangerous night – but at least it had been exciting. At that time I didn't have any friends, either in school or where I lived, and I spent practically every night on my own in my room. Meeting John had been a social experience. Crazy, but that was how I felt.

I decided to dust myself off and move on. It was a tough initiation as first sexual experiences go, but there would be no going back to just fantasising in front of a flickering computer screen. I wasn't put off the idea – I would be doing this again.

Chapter Three

Mark worked in a hospital. Still does, according to his Facebook page. We met in a Yahoo chatroom a few months after my 'date' with Garda John. Once that psycho's ship had sailed, my attention shifted to the man in the green uniform.

By then I was starting to warm to the idea of having a boyfriend. I hadn't had one before and I wanted to try it, plus I liked the idea of having someone who cared about me. Like most teenage girls, I craved the attention of others; a boyfriend would mean a steady stream. That said, I was still open to the idea of meeting up with guys when there was no real promise of a relationship. Even if it turned out to be something short-lived, I would still be the centre of the guy's attention for whatever period of time I spent with him.

I was fifteen and Mark was twenty-six. This

made the entire enterprise illegal, but he didn't seem unduly concerned. We fooled around on webcam; me flashing, teasing and playing with myself while he shifted awkwardly in his seat. As was often the case, he was putty in my hands as soon as the online conversation turned to sex. It was like his brain dropped fifty IQ points as soon as I took off my top.

Mark seemed like a nice guy and I enjoyed chatting with him. He was interesting, and he told lots of funny stories about the crazy shit he saw while working night shifts. He sent me his picture and I was delighted to discover that he was quite good looking: slim with dark-brown hair and a cute smile. His look was almost ruined by a tragic goatee, but at the time I fancied him enough to get past it.

Mark's quirks didn't stop at his fondness for dated facial hair. Most of his hobbies were based around ghosts and other odd supernatural stuff. He spent his free time creeping around old castles and churches with a group of other aficionados recording paranormal activity, or, more likely, mobile phone signals in the belief that they were paranormal activity.

I sometimes struggled to pull together some interesting aspect of my day to tell him about when we chatted online, but I remember his ears pricked up when I mentioned what happened when I met John in person. He told me he thought the way John acted was bang out of order, and that he would never do anything like that. I also told him about something I was beginning to see as an albatross around my neck – the fact that I was still a virgin. This didn't seem to put him off either, especially after I told him there was plenty of other stuff I was willing to do.

My chats with Mark were often interrupted by my ma, who was getting rightly pissed off with me spending all her wages on dial-up internet. My access would usually be restored when I promised to cut down, despite the fact that I would never do anything of the sort. Then, one day, the internet didn't work; my ma had us cut off. It could have been a complete disaster for the fledgling relationship I'd steadily been building with Mark, but for the fact that we had already exchanged phone numbers. So, we replaced dirty online chat with filthy texting.

Mark kept offering to take me for a spin, but I was reluctant. My reticence wasn't because of my misadventures with John; I was long over whatever minor upset that had caused. I felt ready to take another shot at making real the things I talked about online and obsessed about offline. The reason I was hesitant was more to do with the fact that Mark didn't have a car. He rode a motorbike.

Granted cars are not exactly private but I didn't see how we could do any of the things we had been texting each other about without the limited cover of a car. In the end, though, boredom and horniness won out. I also kind of hoped the Ghostbuster might shell out for a hotel or even a B&B if I agreed to meet him.

Mark had a motorbike helmet on when he pulled up at the end of my road. He lifted the visor to say hello, but with night closing in I could only make out part of his face. From what I could gather, though, he was at least the same person as the one in the picture he'd sent. It seems crazy now, but when he handed me a second helmet I didn't think twice. I'd never been on a motorbike before and it looked cool. I pulled on the helmet, threw my leg over the back of the bike and we tore away.

There was little by way of conversation in the car when I met John, but there was absolutely zero chat on the bike. I didn't mind. The excitement of meeting a new guy coupled with the adrenaline buzz from weaving in and out of traffic on the back of a motorbike for the first time was keeping me entertained.

My hopes that he might be taking me to a hotel soon dissipated when he turned into a grubby-looking housing estate about fifteen minutes later. I knew it wasn't where he lived; he had told me his place was on the other side of the city, so I started to feel uneasy. He guided the bike up a path and into a poorly-lit laneway at the end of a row of houses. It was strewn with rubbish and smelled like piss but this, I guessed, was where he had decided he wanted to get down to it. *Fuck it,* I thought, *I'm up for it.*

Mark killed the bike's motor, and when the headlight went off we were in near total darkness. He prised off his helmet, revealing a head of dark, messy hair, a grinning face and his shit goatee. He was around six foot tall, making him at least a foot taller than me.

'So …' I said shyly, hoping he would just go for it.

'So …' he answered, walking towards me and putting his hands around my waist.

The laneway had one of those waist-high metal boxes the council runs phone lines through and he walked me backwards until I was sitting on top of it. He leaned in and kissed me. It was a nice first kiss. He was a good kisser, despite the goatee.

Mark clearly didn't plan on taking things slowly. He stopped kissing me for a moment, stood back and theatrically whipped off his belt. Then he walked back towards me, unbuttoning his jeans and taking out his cock as he went. We started kissing again and he took my hand and placed it on his dick. I started tugging away, freaking out slightly about whether I was doing it right. Meanwhile, he went about liberating as much of me from my clothes as he could. I felt guilty, terrified, thrilled. He pulled down my trousers, taking my knickers with them, and started playing with my clit with his middle finger. I had never been touched by a guy before and it felt like a bolt of electricity darting up my spine. He slipped one finger inside and then another. I was getting wetter and wetter as he worked his fingers in and out and I knew I was going to cum. The urge to scream was almost overwhelming and I had to dig my nails into his back to stop myself from alerting the locals to what was going on in their laneway.

I had cum before while playing with myself but it was nothing like this. I thought I was going to black out. When the jolts of pure bliss subsided I was left tingling all over, and completely soaked. I had no idea I could cum so hard. I was mortified at how wet I was.

'Shit! Sorry!' I said, self-consciously pulling my knickers up.

I don't think he knew what I was talking about at first, and when he finally realised, he seemed amused that I would apologise for cumming.

'That's kind of what I was hoping you would do,' he said, smiling in the darkness.

We kissed again, and this time my full attention was on his cock. He started playing with my tits through my shirt before putting his hands on my shoulders. I knew what he wanted so I dropped to my knees and put the end of his dick in my mouth. He was quite small. Definitely smaller than John the garda. Although I still didn't have much experience and was probably, in all honesty, shit at giving head, Mark was gentlemanly enough to at least not let on. He must have enjoyed himself to some degree because his body soon stiffened. He started thrusting in time with my mouth as I moved back and forth. It was a tad uncomfortable when he hit the back of my throat, but there was no maliciousness in it; he wasn't a tonsil-stabber like John. I was a lot more enthusiastic than I had been on my first attempt at the dark art of giving head, and it paid off – Mark came almost as hard as I had.

At home in bed hours later, I couldn't get my head around what had happened when Mark touched me – how strong the sensation had been. Messing around alone bore no comparison. I had no concept of how sensitive I was until Mark brought me off. I liked Mark, but I quickly concluded that it wasn't all down to him. I was hugely excited about being with a guy and this brought an urgency, an alien thrill that just couldn't be replicated alone. My heart had pounded, my adrenaline had pumped. Blowing on me would have been enough to make me cum. Still, I wasn't over the moon with the way things had gone down. It was fun, but it felt dirty. We didn't have sex, but he had me knicker-less in a laneway. I enjoyed it and would have done it again in a heartbeat, but at the same time I wasn't oblivious to the cheapness of it.

Chapter Four

Mark worked a lot of night shifts, usually finishing after midnight. My ma also did overnight shifts that kept her out of the house until 7 or 8 a.m. This presented an opportunity: I could stay up late (I normally did anyway) and Mark could drop by on his way home from work, while the house was empty. I dropped a hint about how I was home alone when my ma was on shifts, and he dived on it.

I was nervous about Mark coming over. The day before he was due to arrive I scrubbed the life out of my room and put fresh sheets on the bed. There was a distinct possibility I was about to lose my virginity. When the big night came he left the bike at home and turned up in his mother's car. Just as well; he would have looked a tad odd burning down the road on his motorbike in the hospital uniform he arrived in. I was on the edge of my seat the whole night but when the doorbell rang at nearly 3 a.m. I decided to affect a touch of casual sleepiness. Best to not give too much away. The door opened and Mark met me with a broad grin. I led him straight upstairs to my room. I'd picked out a DVD to put on in the background, but I wasn't expecting to see much of it. It was strange having him sitting there on my bed. I'd never had a guy come to my house like this before and even though we had met already, there was still something alien about having him on this side of the computer screen with me. We exchanged the normal hello-how-are-yous and I put on the DVD, but things were happening before the film had even reached the ten-minute mark.

I was slowly inching towards being comfortable in Mark's company, but I was happy to leave it up to him to make the first move. He kissed me, leaning in heavily until I was lying on my back. I had no shoes on, and he yanked my jeans off in one motion before unbuttoning my shirt. Lying there almost naked while he was still wearing his green uniform made me feel self-conscious and a little like I was about to have a medical exam. Happily, it wasn't long before he wriggled out of his own clothes. Within fifteen minutes of Mark's arrival we were wrapped around each other on the bed.

In the end we didn't do anything other than foreplay. He went down on me – another first. Nice as it was, I was more comfortable going down on him than I was having the favour returned. It was a preference that stayed with me for some time, and for years afterwards I classified myself as a 'giver' who wasn't much into getting anything back. There was a key advantage to this inclination – I became very good at giving head.

After we were done fooling around, we lay on the bed spooning, with him behind. Mark was about to make a dickhead of himself, but for the most part he was easy-going, someone you could have a laugh with. We were half chatting and half dozing, when he started playing with my thong. Without any kind of warning, he turned me over slightly and eased his cock straight into my ass. I was in shock that he would do something like that without at least consulting me first, but I let him try it for a short while. Thinking about it now, I don't really know why I didn't kick him out, so to speak. I suppose it was because when you're young you can sometimes do stupid things to impress people, or to make them like you.

With no lubrication, it felt uncomfortable. It wasn't excruciating, but it wasn't pleasurable either. I had heard that anal sex can take a while to get used to, that it gets enjoyable eventually, but I remember thinking that it wasn't a taste I was willing to put the time into acquiring. After a minute or two, I told Mark I wasn't enjoying it and asked him to stop. He whipped his cock back out, somewhat unceremoniously, and we went back to spooning as if nothing had happened. Except now my ass was tingling. It helped that he wasn't exactly hung.

Not long afterwards, Mark ostentatiously checked the time on his mobile phone and announced that he'd better go. He pulled on his clothes, gave me a not particularly passionate peck, told me he'd text me again when he was free and headed out the door. I wasn't too upset about the way he left. To be honest I was happy to be back in my own company. I was pleased with how my first shot at having a boy in my room had gone, despite the fact that I had become one of what must be just a tiny handful of girls on the planet (most others victims of poor aim, I would imagine) to have their anal virginity set sail while their traditional virginity remained intact. I was happy to have had someone drop by. I was happy to be 'seeing' a guy. But mostly I was happy to be doing things I had previously only fantasised about.

Mark started to drop by regularly but it soon became clear the relationship wasn't going to develop beyond the physical. For a start I was coming to realise that I had no real interest in attaching myself to him in any sort of serious way. I still enjoyed spending time with him, but for whatever reason I just wasn't particularly into the guy. Maybe it was that shite goatee.

I didn't have to spell out to Mark how I felt – during his second visit he dropped the bombshell that he had a girlfriend. What we were doing, he explained, was 'just having fun'. I think he expected me to be upset about it, and he seemed slightly put out by the fact that I wasn't.

There was no jealousy there, but it did bother me that Mark would treat his girlfriend that way. I felt bad for her but when it came down to it, he was the one in the relationship; I wasn't betraying anyone. Still, I did feel guilty at times and it made me like him a little bit less. I still enjoyed seeing him and we continued for a while, but it became obvious to both of us that the end was looming. We went back to keeping conversation to a minimum. We would play around, he would cum and then off he'd go into the night, without much in the way of niceties.

Mark was using me. I knew that. I also knew that this was something I was supposed to be concerned about. I think if I was really into him and he was taking advantage of that fact to get his rocks off, then I would have been upset. As it was, with me not being completely sold on the guy anyway, I just wasn't that bothered. I realise it's not exactly a high-minded feminist standpoint, but, as far as I was concerned, I was using him too. There was no real attachment on either side, so he was right – we were just having fun. If I'm honest, the idea of being in a casual, open relationship appealed to me at that age.

It seemed like a grown-up, mature thing to do. My opinion on the subject quickly changed, however, when I met Luke.

Chapter Five

uke was homeless. His parents had kicked him out of the family home for some reason he was never willing to reveal. But rather than being the stereotypical drink- and drug-addled beggar, bedding down in doorways and park benches, he managed to somehow keep his life on a surprisingly even keel. He was in his early twenties and had a lot of friends, so he spent most nights crashed out on someone's sofa. Sometimes, though, his welcome would expire, patience would run out and he would be left with nowhere to go. When faced with a night sleeping rough, Luke would pull together whatever change he had and go to a twenty-four-hour internet café, pay for six or seven hours of computer time and spend the night staring bleary-eyed at a screen. I happened to be burning the midnight oil in our spare room while he was pulling one of his all-nighters in the city centre and we ended up chatting on webcam.

Luke had a shaggy mop of hair and a full-blown beard, but at the time I didn't see this as the hallmarks of the hobo they undoubtedly were. To me, he was a grungy, bohemian, rocker type, and I was fascinated by him. He was easy to talk to, quite charming in fact, and he didn't seem overly concerned by his situation. He looked on the fact that he was a down-and-out as a temporary blip and brushed off my concerns for his well-being. My ma roared from her bedroom at least a half-dozen times that night, telling me to go to bed and finally coming into the room and physically pulling me away from the screen. I was smitten.

That weekend, when my ma was away for a couple of days and the house was empty, I texted Luke to see if he wanted to come around. He told me he was hanging out with a friend of his, a guy called Niall, adding that it would be great if the two of them could drop in. They were at the end of my road within an hour.

I walked out to meet them and was almost struck dumb by the sight of Luke. He told me beforehand that he was tall, but next to me the guy looked like a giant. He had a wiry, gangly frame, a Celtic neck tattoo and was dressed in shabby, goth-ish clothes. He wasn't exactly your typical boyband heartthrob, but at the time I was wrapped.

I said hi, and he introduced me to his far smaller and slightly more neatly dressed friend, Niall. This slightly shifty-looking character was busy knocking back the dregs of a can of Dutch Gold. With the introductions out of the way, Luke asked what I thought about us grabbing a few more beers. 'Sure', I said. There was just one problem, explained Luke. They didn't have any money. 'I've got money,' I said, pulling out a €50 note my ma had given me to pay for food while she was away. We headed to the off-licence.

I was still too young to buy alcohol, so I stood outside while the other pair stocked up. They came out carrying a crate of Dutch Gold and a litre bottle of vodka. 'I hope you don't mind,' said Luke as he handed over the slightly light-looking change. 'I bought twenty smokes while I was in there. It'll save us coming back later.' There was some serious liberty-taking going on, but I was so into the guy that I barely noticed.

It was just starting to get dark when we got back to my place, and once inside the pair flopped onto the sofa. They cracked into the cans while I went off to the kitchen to make up a vodka and Coke. We spent the next few hours getting pissed and talking about music, bands, bars and venues around Dublin. I had been developing an interest in hard rock and metal and Luke, who was very much into that scene, was pouring fuel on the fire. My social life had been so limited that their accounts of nights spent in Dublin's rough-around-the-edges hard rock bar Fibber Magee's seemed almost otherworldly. I wanted to be a part of it.

The few drinks turned into an out-and-out bender and much of what followed blends into a haze. What I do recall is waking up the next morning naked in bed beside Luke, with his mate passed out on the floor beside us.

'Did we do anything last night?' I asked the somehow even more dishevelled-looking Luke.

'Yup,' he groaned by way of reply.

'As in, we had sex?'

'Yeah. You don't remember?' he asked, rolling over to face me.

I had just lost my virginity and I genuinely didn't remember a fucking thing about it. How could that happen? It was another of those things I should have persecuted myself over, but rather than being gutted that I had let something important pass me by, all I felt was relief. I had never been fixated on waiting for some big romantic moment with someone I had been dry-humping for two years to come along before I lost my virginity. The only thing that had held me back was concern about how much it was going to hurt. I wish it had been different when I think about it now, but back then I was glad to have it out of the way without feeling a thing.

While I wasn't too upset at having completely missed the loss of my virginity, I was determined to make the most of my second time. My ma had arranged to go away again the following weekend and I sent a few hopeful texts in the hope of luring Luke to my place while she wasn't around. He didn't take much convincing. In fact he jumped at the offer. Better still, he promised to leave his mate at home.

Butterflies fluttered in my stomach as the big day approached and I spent the final hours before his arrival scrubbing my bedroom and agonising over what to wear. He turned up carrying a bag of cans and we spent our first hour alone together working our way through it. The butterflies hadn't dissipated with Luke's arrival and I hoped a few drinks might put some steel in my spine. Luke was unusual in that he was as easy to talk to in person as he was online. He had an effortless charm about him that completely won me over.

'Okay maybe we should take it easy,' said Luke, suddenly taking my can from my hand and putting in on the floor next to my bed. 'We can't have you forgetting your second time, too.'

He was so tall compared to me that when he leaned in to kiss me I had to tilt my head right back to reciprocate. I felt like my neck was about to snap until he eased me back onto the bed so I was lying flat on my back. The room spun as he kissed me. It felt like the he was slowing the whole world down. He unbuttoned my shirt with one hand, and I self-conciously wiggled my way out of it. Seconds later, we were both completely naked. I wasn't cold, but I bristled and trembled as he ran his fingers across my body.

Luke retrieved a condom from his jeans and slipped it on in seconds. It left me wondering how many girls he'd been with, and how I was going to compare. He eased himself between my legs, a slight smile breaking across his face. I felt a sudden pang of fear as he guided the tip of his cock inside me. I was worried that a girl's second time might be just as painful as her first. My breathing quickend as he entered me. It wasn't painful, but he felt ominously big. That was hardly surprising; as he lay on top of me my face ran to about the mid-point of his chest.

I closed my eyes as his pace quickened – I couldn't believe I was really doing it. I had dreamed about having sex for so long that I wondered whether it would ever happen. When it finally did and I ended up not being able to remember it, I thought I must be cursed. Now, finally, it was really happening; and with a guy I was crazy about.

'Are you okay?' Luke asked, sounding genuninely concerned.

'Sure, I'm okay,' I said, attempting to brush it off.

But I wasn't just okay. I felt amazing. Waves of pleasure rippled through my body and I dug my nails into his back. He began to speed up his strokes, slamming the full length of his dick into me. I could see by the expression on his face that he was enjoying it almost as much as I was. He was fucking me hard but although it began to hurt a little, I was going to take it.

Luke suddenly pulled out and climbed off me, snapping me out of a liquid reverie. I thought something had gone wrong; it was all new to me, but when he casually flipped me over and positioned himself behind me I realised what he wanted. I reached behind and gripped his dick, pushing it into my pussy. I was so wet that it slipped inside easily.

He felt brutally strong as he began fucking me fast and hard. He had done all the warming up he was going to do and I couldn't stifle my moans any longer. I could hear his breath quickening as he pounded on me, grabbing a handful of my hair and roughly wrenching my head back. A familiar feeling of euphoria began to envelop me, burning from the pit of my stomach to tips of my fingers and toes. It reminded me of what I felt that night in the alleyway with Mark but far, far stronger. I felt like I was going to black out as his body stiffened – Luke was going to cum too. Then it happened – the room swam and then disappeared, and I was in another world. All that existed were me, him and the ferocious, all-encompassing pleasure we both felt.

I heard myself screaming but it sounded like it was coming from someone else in some other place. The room slowly returned as we collapsed panting onto the bed, my body trembling as the final pulses of pleasure disapated.

Some people are left disappointed by their first time having sex, but I wasn't. It was incredible. It was better than I could have imagined. I decided there and then that whatever happened, and whatever direction my life took, sex was going to be a big part of it. I had found something I loved, and I was going to make the most of it.

I saw Luke regularly after that and he quickly became my first major crush. We would meet up and hang out around the city centre and he introduced me to more of his rocker mates. But there was only one place we wanted to spend our time – the bedroom.

Whenever my ma wasn't around and Luke was free (Luke was always free) he would sneak around to my place. The pre-sex conversations gradually got shorter and shorter until it got to the point where we would dive on each other as soon as the door closed behind him.

After a few weeks, I started to notice something about Luke. He liked to throw his weight around when we had sex. He would put his giant hands around my waist, scoop me up and then slam me roughly onto the bed. He made the most of the height difference, too. He enjoyed pinning me against the wall and fucking me while my I wrapped myself around him, my feet half a yard off the floor.

The more we had sex, the braver he became and these little kinks came to the fore more often. He pulled my hair. He slapped my ass he fucked me from behind. He bit gently on my nipples. It wasn't a problem for me. In fact, I couldn't get enough of it. We never actually spoke about the direction our sex life was going in, but I did my best to encourage him.

I would moan on cue to let him know I was enjoying myself. There were never any props, costumes or safe words brought into play but I think these early experiences planted a seed.

Although there was a lot of it, the relationship felt like it was about more than sex. He had this casual, laid-back cynicism about the world that I just loved. I was really into the way he dressed and the fact that he had such an extreme, alien lifestyle attracted me further. I wanted in. I copied the clothes and make-up his female friends would wear and listened to the music they talked about.

It was becoming pretty obvious that I was falling for Luke. I thought about him when he wasn't there and fussed over him when he was. I cringe at the thought of what a sappy teen I was back then but I even started making the guy food before he left. Sex and sandwiches. Luke had a sweet deal.

As much as I liked Luke, I never told anyone about him. I didn't exactly have a gaggle of girlfriends to sit and chat about boys with, but I didn't tell my family, either. I had kept everything I did online so separate from my school and home life that it seemed natural that I would keep my first relationship from them, too. I was starting to come out of myself a little and I liked the person I was turning into when I was with Luke and his friends. But this new me was someone my family didn't know. At home and school, I was still the introverted wall flower with nothing to say. So it just seemed easier to compartmentalise.

Although I made it as clear as I could to Luke that I was crazy about him, I was never really sure how he felt about me – until one day when he asked me to meet him in a pool hall we went to once in a while. When I arrived, he was standing with a group of his friends, with his arms around a girl. I was stunned. I thought I was going to burst into tears on the spot. I realised then that although my virginity hadn't meant all that much to me, I had hoped it meant something to him. To top it off, she was skinny and prissy-looking: exactly the type of girl I'd hoped he wasn't interested in. I turned and left without saying a word to him. I blubbed myself to sleep that night and promised myself I would never speak to him again.

I was so upset that I got in touch with one of the few people I knew outside Luke's circle of mates – my ghost-busting, ass-fucking, hospital-worker friend. I called and told him what happened – I had lost my virginity to some prick that made a fool out of me. Mark was surprisingly understanding, and he offered to swing by and take me for a spin. It was evening when he turned up in his ma's car and just about dark when we pulled into a car park next to the beach. It was the same one I had gone to with John a couple of years previously. I sobbed through the story of what happened, while Mark sat and listened. He put his arms around me and before I knew it, we were kissing. I didn't plan or want any of it; I just wanted to talk. I felt overwhelmed, confused and desperate for affection after what had happened, and Mark took full advantage. To cut a long story short, that vulture became the second person I had sex with, and then I never saw him again.

To this day, I still find it strange that he never showed any interest in being my first. It seems slightly implausible that he would have held back because he didn't want the pressure of being the first person I slept with, given that he was happy to be the first to fuck me up the ass. That said, I don't think it's a coincidence that he suddenly wanted to have sex with me when he found out I had lost my virginity.

Fast running out of people in the real world I could talk to, I turned again to the internet. It was shortly afterwards, when I was still licking my wounds and wondering whether every man on the planet was a predatory prick, that a message popped up on my screen from a guy called Matthew. Within months, we were completely in love with each other.

Chapter Six

One of the things that set Matthew apart from the other guys I had been with was the fact that he was my own age. I had just turned sixteen and he was a year older. The other thing that stood out about him was that he was a red-head. While this wouldn't be an attribute I'd look for, with his sallow skin and glistening green eyes, he was probably the best-looking ginger I'd ever seen.

We hit it off straight away and I shoved aside all the other guys I chatted with online. But there was one major problem: he was from, and lived in, London. I knew it would be difficult, but I was hopeful that we could figure out a way of meeting.

After what had happened with Luke, I was very much tuned in to whether or not Matthew reciprocated my feelings for him. Insofar as I could tell, he was as into me as I was into him. He suggested a visit to

Ireland, and we were soon laying plans for his visit. My ma was lining up another of her occasional jaunts down the country and by then, my older sister had already moved out. She had moved into her own apartment with her two kids.

This meant that as soon as my ma headed off, I could put Matthew up. He finally arrived, and we couldn't keep our hands off each other. Aside from the whole red-head thing, he was even better looking in person. The months of waiting had charged the sexual tension to maximum and I wanted him so badly it was almost unbearable. We were in my bedroom within seconds and I was soon frantically ripping off his clothes to reveal a toned, heavily tattooed body. We attacked each other, fucking hard and fast. It felt like blasts of electricity were surging between the two of us. We were both so turned on that it was over quickly, but I didn't mind. We were soon diving into round two.

We spent the whole weekend together, rarely venturing from the bedroom. We had an incredible time together. Being with him felt completely different from my earlier experiences, which were cheap and nasty by comparison. I kept him entirely to myself that weekend and he barely set foot outside the door during his entire stay. He flew home without having been introduced to anyone. I would have liked to have paraded him around, but I felt like there was still a stigma attached to meeting someone on the internet. I thought shipping someone over from the UK might have looked desperate.

Nonetheless things were looking up for me. I had come off the medication and, at the doctor's suggestion, I got a job to keep myself occupied. He felt that working in an environment in which I would be dealing with people regularly would help me deal with my shyness and bring me out of my shell. My ma was pleased, too, because although she had encouraged me to stay in school, she was of the opinion that if I was going to be skipping practically every day, I should be out earning a wage instead. I found work in Dublin Airport and, from dealing with customers all day, I became far less socially awkward. The puppy fat I had stressed about so much was falling away, and having more money meant I wasn't as limited in what I could do and where I could go. The only downside was the fact that I was watching flights taking off for the UK all day every day. I really, really wanted to be on them. Eventually, after bouncing the idea back and forth online, I decided to visit Matthew in London.

Both my parents were dead against the idea of their teenage daughter flying to the UK to shack up with a guy they hadn't met, but that wasn't going to stop me. Flights were cheap, and after the first trip went well I started going over every time I could get a weekend off. Matthew and I were getting more and more attached and even though I was making it over to see him quite often, the goodbyes were still heart-wrenching. We needed a long-term solution. Matthew was in the middle of a welding apprenticeship, so he couldn't up-sticks and leave home. There was only one thing for it: I would have to be the one to do the leaving.

I moved into Matthew's bedroom in his family's home in a rough part of London's East End. The honeymoon period didn't last long. It soon became clear that this wasn't going to be the happy love nest we had hoped it might be. Matthew lived with his mother, father, two sisters and one brother. The house was cramped as it was, and my being there wasn't helping. To make things worse, my increasingly frantic efforts to find a job and at least contribute something were a disaster. I couldn't find work anywhere. Weeks and then months passed without so much as an interview.

It didn't help that Matthew's father was a complete psycho. He was addicted to depression medication and was a chronic alcoholic. He was on a transplant list for a new liver, but even his dire health condition didn't stop him drinking. His liver was so bad that every time he forced any kind of alcohol into his system, he would become violently ill. But he was nothing if not dedicated, and he went out and got hammered as often as he could. He hadn't worked in decades; the nearest thing he had to a job was a long-standing involvement with a criminal gang. The scumbag had even brought his son into the fold. By the time Matthew was sixteen his dad was entering him into illegal bare-knuckle boxing matches.

Matthew turned his back on that part of his life when his father was attacked and almost killed. His dad had found out that another gang member was molesting his own daughter. He had threatened to tell the police, and the guy's response was to cut Matthew's father's throat from ear-to-ear and leave him for dead at the side of the road. He was found and taken to hospital before he'd bled to death, but he'd been left with a lumpy, stomach-turning scar that ran along the underside of his jawline. Once healed, it was just another for his collection; the chewed-up wreck of a man had scars all over him.

Matthew didn't often talk about the things he had done when he was younger. He said this was because he had moved on and didn't see the need, but there was more to it than that. He didn't want to talk about it because it brought up some serious issues – in particular issues with his father, who had got him involved in the gang-related stuff. But Matthew was a reformed character. Even his da had turned away from much of what he had been involved in, although a carved-up alcoholic who could barely function as a human being probably wasn't in very high demand among the criminal fraternity anyway. Instead, Matthew's father had taken up smoking weed. I think it helped mellow him out. Even so, peace never reigned for long in that house.

Matthew's father had separated from his mother for a couple of years and he had fathered a son while on the loose. While I was there, this son tracked him down and turned up at the door one day. That triggered a particularly vicious row – the son was clean-cut, handsome, healthy-looking ... and a policeman.

When Matthew was unexpectedly let go by the company that was training him, things came to a head. Matthew's father completely turned on me. I had managed to get a job stacking shelves and once I had paid my debts I started handing up money to the family. But it was too late. Matthew's dad had already decided he wanted me out. He had a way of manipulating Matthew into doing what he wanted, and our relationship started to sour. I was heartbroken, but I knew it was time to leave. I should have gone straight home but I couldn't face it. The things I didn't like about home had played almost as big a part in my wanting to go to England as my love for Matthew had. My parents, probably relieved that I was about to finally remove myself from the slummy, dysfunctional life I'd dived into, were as understanding as ever. I had an aunt and uncle living in Luton. They said I could stay there for a while, and even get paid a few quid a week if I looked after my young cousins.

My da was good enough to send money to my aunt for rent, and I got the occasional shift working in the catering business she owned. I still travelled to London to meet up with Matthew at weekends, but it was becoming clear that the relationship had had its chance. In all, I spent a year and five months in England – London for a year, Luton for five months. As much as I tried to hide it, I was absolutely miserable in Luton and with a return to London not on the cards, I eventually decided to come home to Dublin. Matthew was as distraught as I was when the time came for me to leave England for good, but things weren't going to change, not enough to justify me staying there anyway.

On reflection I think that trip was good for me. I was desperate to leave Ireland because I thought my problems were due to where I was, and that if I moved somewhere else everything would be fine. I think I needed that time away to see that the place wasn't the problem. When I got home, I was determined that I wouldn't just exist anymore. I was going to start living.

Chapter Seven

I returned home to difficult living arrangements. My ma had bought a small place for herself in the Kilkenny countryside. She still worked Monday to Friday as a live-in carer in Dublin, but at weekends and holidays she headed off to the midlands. My sister was still living in her own place with her kids. My da's mother wasn't well at the time, so he moved in to her place to help look after her. A stay in darkest rural Kilkenny was out of the question so I had to move in with my da. Living with your dad and sick nan is not exactly conducive to a carefree lifestyle, but I didn't have a whole lot of options, not least because I had decided to go back and finish school.

It wasn't all bad. I was happy to be home and I was looking forward to getting stuck into my studies. I thought of myself as a worldly-wise well-travelled individual after my time in England. I had lived abroad, worked different jobs, loved and lost. School no longer held any fear for me and I actually looked forward to the social side of things.

My dad stumped up the cash for me to study for the Leaving Certificate exams in a well-known private college. He had a few extra quid from the sale of the old family home, and he was happy to have something he saw as worthwhile to spend it on.

I arrived on my first day, impeccably prepared. I had every book and document I might possibly need, and I was also armed to teeth with pens, pencils, highlighters, protractors, folders, binders and stacks of other paraphernalia unlikely to ever be needed. My meticulousness spilled over into my classes, and in my first term I was shocked to find myself getting As in literally every subject. Despite growing up in a housing estate with a garden you couldn't grow a carrot in, I even managed to get an A in agricultural science.

My borderline obsessive-compulsive diligence was working to my advantage, but it all came crashing down when I got sick shortly after the first term ended.

I missed two weeks, and found it difficult to get back into the swing of things. My absence had left a hole in my carefully tagged and highlighted notes. I was disappointed and I came to the sullen conclusion that my plans to immerse myself in academia were irreparably ruined.

Fuck it, I thought, suddenly realising how wafer thin my motivation had been.

I thought I had been looking forward to starting school again, while I was still in England, but I think I was really just looking forward to getting back home.

It sucked, and not just for me. My long-suffering dad had bought me a study desk and he was thrilled that I was making a go of it. He was shelling out €6,000 for each of the two years I would study at the college, and extra for my books and alarming stationery demands. He really tried, but at the time I didn't appreciate it.

Of course, it didn't help that my social life had kicked up a gear.

My school had a fearsome reputation as a haven for stuck-up cubs of Celtic Tiger Ireland, but I found this to be somewhat undeserved. While some of the students did fall into the nose-in-the-air category, there were plenty of others in a similar situation to me – children of normal parents who had to sacrifice in order to give their kids a second chance.

Internet 'dating' had been off the agenda while I was in a relationship, and even once home, especially now that I had a new social outlet, it hadn't regained its appeal. This was happening at a time when it was becoming more accessible because of the arrival of the first wave of social media sites. It was also becoming more socially acceptable, and in a move that surprised us all, my da unveiled a new girlfriend he had met online. She was from the Philippines, but had been working in Ireland for some time. They completely fell for each other and they eventually got married. This theme continued when my mam met her long-term boyfriend on a dating site. The most effective way of turning a teenage girl off anything is to get her parents to do it and I came to the conclusion that searching the internet for a boyfriend or girlfriend was, well, a bit sad. From now on, I decided, I wanted to meet people the old fashioned way.

I slotted easily into the school's social scene. I was older than most of the other students in my form, which I think helped. There were plenty of rich kids floating around, but I even managed to get on well with them. It wasn't that I was going out of my way to be particularly social, but I found that others would often invite me into their company. It might just have been my age – or maybe it was because my peroxide blonde hair and growing collection of piercings and tattoos made me stand out a little.

My college was located slap bang in Dublin city centre, and I started hanging out with a group of other students in a nearby city park. I wasn't the only one willing to skip classes, and we would occupy ourselves by drinking naggins of vodka, cans of Bulmers or bottles of Jägermeister, before stumbling back to class. It started as an occasional day-time piss-up in the park, but quickly turned into something regular. It was worsened by the fact that, as a nineteen-year-old, I was fully entitled to stroll into whatever pub I liked and order a drink.

I wanted to go to Fibber's, the rock pub I had been borderline obsessed with in my mid-teens. I liked many of the people I knew from school, but I wasn't particularly close to any of them. They were all underage and they didn't have the piercing/tattoo/ heavy metal fixation I did. Although the thought of such a move would have once crippled me with anxiety, I decided I would go out on my own.

The idea of going into a pub alone was scary, but a few quick drinks at home helped me over the line. When it came to it, it wasn't as nerve-wracking as I thought it might be. Fibber's attracted a laid-back, unconventional crowd. I got the impression that while a girl on her own would have raised eyebrows in a lot of pubs, nobody in Fibber's gave a shite. The drink was cheap and I found the people unpretentious and easy to talk too. My first night was fairly uneventful, but I liked the place and started going regularly. Smelly rockers might appear hostile, but they're friendlier than they look.

Every Saturday and most Fridays I would wander in and order a vodka and Diet Coke before strolling outside to the smoking area. There would invariably be a scruffy collection of people happy to share conversations about music, tattoos and piercings. I had been drinking in Fibber's for about a month when I met Anna. I arrived on a Friday night after a hard day at school and she was sitting at the bar by herself. We got chatting while the barman was getting my drink. She was close to my height – about 5 foot three – with bleached blonde hair. She was wearing a pulled-tight corset, black platform shoes and deep-red lipstick. She was from Norway, and although she was the first person I'd ever met from that country, she somehow looked typically Norwegian, I thought. She asked if I was there on my own and when I said yes, she explained why she was too.

Anna was twenty-four and had moved to Ireland to be with her Irish boyfriend. She got a job as a computer programmer and all was well for the first two years of their relationship. They spent all their time together, but this meant her circle of friends never developed beyond his. Then they split up and she was left alone in a city where she had no family and no real friends. Once she got over the break-up, she decided to start going out. She was into the rock scene, so Fibber's became the first bar of the rest of her life. I discovered something else about Anna that night: the girl could drink. We spent the night chatting, running outside to smoke weed down an alleyway beyond the glare of the bouncers and fending off the attentions of the guys who occasionally approached us. We had a blast.

Anna and I traded numbers and got in touch ahead of the following weekend. We met up again that Saturday and we were soon regular drinking buddies. Our nights out began with warm up drinks in either my place or hers and, once loaded up, we would head into the city centre. We tried a few other bars and clubs, but Fibber's was our local. I loved the place. The people who went there didn't obsess over their appearance like they did in practically every other bar within a five mile radius of Dublin city centre. It gave the place a relaxed, fun vibe and I was comfortable there. Nobody was out to judge, and it became a place where I felt I could let my hair down and enjoy myself.

A side-effect of that relaxed atmosphere was that there was often a dearth of girls among the crowd so Anna and I got a lot of attention. We would spend chunks of each night fending off unwanted suitors, but it was all part of the fun. However, there were occasions when someone I did take an interest in approached us. I was still living at home with my dad, but if a guy I liked asked me back to his place, I didn't always refuse. We were drinking a lot, smoking a lot and I often woke up with little or no recollection of what happened the night before. It was messy, drink-fuelled and hedonistic, but it was a happy time.

Crucially, I was getting attention – normal attention from guys who found me attractive. I wasn't luring these guys by stripping on a webcam. I was just going out and having fun, and because I was happy and enjoying myself, people wanted to spend time with me. I knew at the time my drinking was getting serious, but despite this I felt like I was becoming someone I wanted to be. Drink had a positive role in this. It was giving me the confidence to do more of the things I wanted to do; it was stripping away my inhibitions. A few vodkas made me chattier, more outgoing and, I discovered, quite funny. I seemed to effortlessly fire out witty remarks that left the people around me doubled up laughing.

It made me wonder why I couldn't do the same when I was sober. I mean, I said some funny shit when I was drunk, but drink wasn't putting any new information into my head. It was all already in there, but for some reason I didn't have the capacity to pull the trigger when I was sober.

As the weeks passed, I could feel myself coming further out of my shell with every night out. The adventurousness that had up until then only manifested itself in my online antics began to come to the fore. I wanted to experiment. I wanted to try new things and one new thing in particular: I wanted to kiss a girl.

It first occurred to me when I was sitting in Fibber's with Anna and a girl walked in with two male friends. She was short with liquid-black hair platted and tied up at the back. She looked Latin, and her body was gym-bunny tight. What really stood out about this girl, though, was her round, full lips. As soon as I saw her I just ached to see if they were as soft as they looked. I spent much of the rest of the night snatching glimpses of her, and when our eyes finally met she smiled at me. I fancied myself as quite the wild child by then, but even with a skin full of drink I couldn't bring myself to go and speak to her. She left with her friends around midnight, and I never saw her again.

The next day, and for weeks afterwards, I bitterly regretted not approaching her. I was furious with myself for allowing self-doubt to stop me from doing what I wanted to do. I had no way of knowing if the girl would have been interested in anything – I didn't even know if I was interested in taking it further – but I'd had nothing to lose from saying hello. But fear of rejection, or of looking silly, had kept me glued to my seat. It was a feeling I faced too often when I was growing up, and I had hoped it was behind me. It came as a shock to discover that I was still clinging onto my inhibitions. I made a decision: they would have to go.

My sudden interest in girls didn't wane over the weeks that followed, and in a drunken haze I had my first girl-on-girl kiss. I had built it up in my mind beforehand, but it was a bit of a non-event. Straight girls kiss each other for dramatic effect, or to wind up any guys who might be watching, all the time. It was more playful than anything. I don't remember much about the girl beyond the fact that she was straight. It wasn't a defining moment for me – there was no bolt of lightning or moment of clarity. There was no real sexual tension to it either; we were just messing around. What I do remember is concluding that girls are better kissers than guys.

The most significant thing about that kiss wasn't that it was important in and of itself, it was that it was an indicator of how far I had come. The shy, unsure girl was being left behind. This was another marker on my road.

I was spending a significant proportion of my school day pissed, either from the night before or because of lunchtime benders, and my drinking habits were obliterating any hope I had of carrying my promising early form in school through to a good Leaving Cert result. Even worse, the spectacular decline in my performance didn't go unnoticed. I remember a well-meaning maths teacher asking if she could see me at the end of the last class before lunch. I was reluctant to hand my free time over to anything even remotely associated with school, but she was so eye-wateringly earnest in her concern for me that I agreed.

She thought it would be a good idea to bring me to a pub to talk about my problems, and we headed to a bar just across the road from the college. She was just a couple of years older than I was, and she was evidently preparing to have a stab at reaching out on a human level, rather than on a teacher/student one. She treated me to lunch, and when we finished eating she asked me if everything was okay.

'Is there something going on we need to know about?' she asked, her voice dipped in genuine concern. I wanted to tell her the truth – that everything was great. I finally had a social life worthy of the name. In alcohol, I had found a magical formula that blasted away anxiety and shyness, leaving behind the cool, confident, funny young girl I wanted to be. I actually felt sorry for her. She didn't even know me but she seemed quite cut up about the fact that my grades were sliding. I decided that because she had probably already guessed that drink figured in the equation, I might as well level with her. I told her about how I had started going out drinking a lot more. I decided to leave out how brilliant I thought it was. She asked me where I went, and when I told her I was a regular at

Fibber's she looked even more concerned. 'That place is bad for you,' she said, leaning back in her chair.

As it turned out, she and her boyfriend used to get drunk in Fibber's regularly while she was in college. Their drinking very nearly got out of control. It had almost ruined her career before it even got started. Before leaving, I promised I would try and rein it in and focus on school a bit more.

In short, I did neither.

Chapter Eight

'So,' asked Anna with a mischievous smile. 'Are we on?'

Anna had just explained how she had discovered a fetish night held in a private room upstairs in a Dublin city-centre pub. It was held on the last week of each month and she had been there with her ex-boyfriend. She wanted to go again, and was wondering if I would go with her. Her suggestion hardly came as a surprise – the girl had more corsets than a Jane Austen heroine and I had never seen her outdoors without a layer of vampish make-up. I had to admit, the fetish night sounded interesting. I had no idea anything like that went on in Dublin and I was immediately curious. 'Sure,' I said. 'Sounds like fun.'

Anna explained that the organisers of the event enforced a strict dress code – anyone hoping to get past the door would have to be clad in leather, rubber, big heels and short skirts. We could stop short of a ball gag, but taking part wasn't something we could do by halves. So, my Norwegian fetishist friend and I went shopping. Anna already had more suitable clothing than she needed, so we were mostly shopping for my outfit. There was something very girly about the experience – even if we were shopping for gimp-wear – but I enjoyed it. It helped build the anticipation and made the night itself something to really look forward too.

I had until then avoided skirts like the plague but, under pressure from Anna, I decided to take the plunge and buy a leather mini. I remember looking at it in the changing room mirror, pulling it down at the sides and thinking about how it bore absolutely no relation to any item of clothing I had ever bought before. But I liked it. I bought a tight black top to go with it, and stopped off in Ann Summers for a scandalous pair of knee-high leather boots.

Before we left, Anna made one final addition to the ensemble – she picked out a pair of pink and black leather handcuffs connected to a sort of leash.

'I'll be the dom and you'll be the submissive,' said Anna with a sexy smile. 'I'll own you for the night.'

'Yes, mistress,' I said.

We met for a quick drink beforehand in a bar packed with Guinness-drinking seniors and work-worn dockers. Anna walked into the bar casually swinging her leash and dressed in her trade-mark corset-and-red-lipstick combo and a pair of black platform boots. We ordered a round and grabbed a seat, but we could barely hear each other over the sound of jaws dropping open. While it was amusing to see how the pub-goers reacted to us, I was keen to get to the event, so we finished up our drinks and made our way to the venue.

One of the organisers was manning the entrance at the bottom of the stairs that led up to the event, checking costumes and taking the cover charge. I recognised him as a regular from the rock scene. He was slim and well over six foot, with long black hair. He was dressed in a bizarre outfit made up of a black cowboy hat, a black string vest and a pair of leather trousers. His arms were covered in tattooed images of devils, upside-down crosses and various other pieces of gothic nastiness. He was impressed enough with our outfits to let us in, but Anna decided to click her leash onto my cuffs for the full effect anyway. The guy struggled to take the smile off his face as he took the entry fee and waved us upstairs.

I was nervous walking upstairs, but not unpleasantly so. I was excited to be trying something new. I couldn't wait to see what everyone else was wearing and to see how they reacted to our outfits. The room was small, with a bar in the far corner, and although we were early, some thirty people had already pushed inside. Most were chatting away normally, seemingly unaware of the fact that so many of them were dressed like something out of a fetish porno. I noticed that the organiser on the stairs wasn't the only person I recognised. There were quite a few familiar faces. Thinking about it now, it wasn't a coincidence that the people who drank in rocker bars would end up at an event like that. Sure, there were plenty of closet cases wandering around who probably worked as bankers or gardaí, but they had to be a bit more circumspect about turning up for an event like that. Rockers went out of their way to look as disreputable as they possibly could, so there was little point in hiding an interest in fetishism where there was one.

We went to the bar, ordered a drink and looked around at Dublin's sexual deviant set. Although everyone seemed to be having a good time, when I remember that night one guy in particular sticks in my mind. He was middle-aged with a shaved head and slightly protruding ears. He was sitting at a table alone, looking into his pint. He was wearing a full-blown gimp outfit, only minus the mask. What really stuck out about him though, was how lonely he looked. He was just sitting there, hoping someone would come and talk to him. I kept glancing in his direction that night, wondering if he would make a friend, but he remained alone. I didn't approach him. Then, sometime around midnight, he was gone.

Despite the arresting sight of the lonely gimp, we had a great night. They looked terrifying, but the sadomasochistic crowd turned out to be a great group of people to hang out with. Anna and I played up to our dominant/submissive personas. She led me around the room and introducing me as her slave to the party-goers we spoke to. Anna was in her element and there was something about submitting to another person's whims that really appealed to me. Although Anna and I were purely friends and I wasn't in any way attracted to her, I was massively turned on whenever she yanked my chain, ordered me around or playfully slapped my ass. Being surrounded by these people and being with Anna when she was fully in dominatrix mode was a little scary, but the adrenaline just added to the pleasure.

On reflection I think the seed of this particular kink had been planted years before. Right from my first sexual experiences, I had, wittingly or unwittingly, been adopting passive roles with the guys I was with. I would imagine a lot of girls would have been turned off sex for life if her first experiences had involved gagging on a garda's cock or being fucked in the ass by a guy ten years her senior, but I had been left wanting more. I had grown to love it when a guy took charge in the bedroom, and I was far more into giving head than getting it. I just never connected these sexual preferences with S&M, a slightly deviant sexual predilection. This was something I wanted to explore further.

The party wound to a close at kicking out time so

we went to the George – a well-known gay nightclub. I had never been to a gay bar before but the night had a sexual awakening-type theme to it so another first couldn't hurt. The club was bigger than I expected with a large, already-heaving dance floor. It was filled mostly with gay guys, but there was no shortage of gay girls, either. Anna jokingly asked if I saw anyone I liked, before heading towards the bar. Even before we got our hands on our first drink we were approached by some scary-looking lesbians. Many lived up to the stereotype: short hair, men's clothes and gruff attitudes. Others were completely indistinguishable from any straight girl you would see on the street. I found myself wondering who among the women in my life were secretly gay, and I occasionally scanned the crowd for a glimpse of a familiar face. Our daring outfits meant a steady stream of would-be suitors came in our direction and we eventually had to pretend to be a couple. We weren't being hassled – the crowd in the George was great craic – but saying we were together meant we didn't have to explain why we were in a gay club. Anna was straight, our relationship was platonic and nothing was going to happen, but we enjoyed flirting and dancing with each other in the sexiest way we could manage in our over-high shoes. In the end, we went home separately, exchanging nothing beyond a friendly kiss on the cheek.

We met again on Sunday, and I turned up for school on Monday with a spirit-crushing hangover. I came armed with a naggin of vodka emptied into a Ribena bottle. If I could make it to lunchtime without taking a bite out of anyone, I decided, I would straighten my head out by throwing it back. As it turned out, I would need it sooner than I thought. I was stumbling towards the door at the end of my first class when my friendly, interfering maths teacher called me back for a 'quick word'. She had arranged an appointment for me with the school counsellor.

'You've been pencilled in for 10 a.m., so you'll need to go over to his office now,' she said, her sympathetic expression starting to look a bit patronising.

'No problem,' I said, taking a swing from my bottle of Ribena.

I had to sit like a bold child on a plastic chair

outside the counsellor's office and I resented it. I resented the whole school. My hangover was making me see everything in a harsh, bitter light and I had to fight the urge to walk out and never come back. I consoled myself with a few more gulps.

The door swung open and an overweight, fifty-something guy with a beard and a kindly face waved me inside. I sat down, and he began to run through the script he breaks out for troubled teens. It bore some remarkable similarities to the spiel I had gotten from my maths teacher the previous week. He explained how concerns about my performance had been expressed to him, and that he wanted to make sure everything was all right. He asked if everything was okay at home, if something was bothering me and if I was mixing okay with the other students.

'It's not just about study,' he said. 'It's important to have social outlets, too.'

'Really, I'm fine,' I said with as much gentle conviction as I could manage. 'My social outlets were probably the problem, but I've been getting back to the books a lot more recently, so I'm sure you'll be hearing about an improvement from my teachers soon enough.'

'I'm glad to hear it,' he said.

With that, I took a final gulp from my Ribena bottle, thanked him for his time and headed for the door.

Unfortunately, fobbing off my dad wasn't quite as easy. I knew I was going off the rails, and the late nights, not to mention the occasional overnight absences, meant he soon realised it too. He tried leaping out of bed to confront me when I fell in the door in the early hours of the morning, but he soon realised that there was little point – by the next morning I rarely remembered even speaking to him. Next he tried tackling me the morning after, but picking a fight with a hungover, hormonal teenage girl, he quickly discovered, was like poking a wasp nest with a stick. We had screaming rows that invariably ended with one or other of us storming out of the house with the histrionic slamming of a door.

I sometimes felt bad about my relationship with my dad. He was putting me up, supporting me and paying for my second chance at an education, and I wasn't exactly embracing the opportunity he was handing me on a plate. But teenage girls can be selfish, and I tended to see him as an obstacle to my having a good time rather than someone who was trying to help me.

My night-time life crashed into my day-time routine in other ways, too. On one occasion, I was walking with some school mates through the city centre during lunch, when one of the girls pointed out a bizarre-looking individual strutting down the road towards us. He was tall, and wearing a leather cowboy hat, tight black jeans, a mesh top and what looked like some sort of samurai mask. The rest of the group were giggling at his ridiculous get-up, but I was struck dumb – I knew him. It was the organiser of the S&M event I had been to with Anna. I prayed he wouldn't spot me, but no such luck. He walked straight up to me, pulled off his mask and threw his arms around me and said, 'Hey, how are you? Did you have a good time the other night?'

The others stayed silent until he was gone, at which point they unleashed a barrage of where-in-the-name-of-God-do-you-know-him-froms.

I couldn't really explain that he was an organiser at the fetish event I went to, so I just shrugged my shoulders and tried not to look embarrassed.

'I dunno,' I said. 'I just know him from around.'

I somehow made it through two years of schooling without being kicked out for turning up pissed. In the run-up to my final exams, I even eased off on nights out and cracked the books. Irish had been a particular problem for me, and I focused a lot of what little studious energy I had on making sure I didn't fail it catastrophically. I even signed up for extra Irish periods. The exams themselves were a turgid affair, but I was feeling particularly shite ahead of my Irish exam. At first I thought I was just anxious, but when I started to involuntarily double up ten minutes into the paper, I knew it was something more serious. Alarmingly, I felt like I needed to pee – even though I had just been to the toilet. I excused myself and went to the bathroom. I was hit with a staggeringly painful burning sensation when I tried to go again. I was big on condom use but the amount of drink I consumed before going home with someone meant I couldn't be sure there hadn't been a slip.

With my cramps worsening, I knew I wasn't going

to get through the exam. After going back inside and explaining my symptoms to the examiner through shuddering stabbing pains in my lower abdomen, I was rushed to hospital. After the extraction of various bodily fluids and several rounds of uncomfortable prodding, I was finally given a diagnosis – I had cystitis. Better than an STD, but it meant I would be taking the remainder of my exams filled to the gills with painkillers, antibiotics and anti-inflammatories.

My results were not spectacular but given the circumstances, I thought I did well. They were far better than I, and probably my parents and teachers, thought they would be. I passed, and even got a couple of honours. I hadn't put in anywhere near as much work as I should have, basically because I didn't really give a shit. That didn't change on results day – I could have handled a fail. My da, on the other hand, was delighted. He had shelled out thousands of euro to get me that exam result and, given my somewhat questionable lifestyle choices, he must have thought I was going to crash and burn.

The students planned to hit the town on results night, but I didn't much fancy tagging along. I had something else in mind. I got in touch with Anna, and with my da out (celebrating probably), she arrived at mine with a bottle of vodka and a big smile. After working our way through half the bottle and jointly marvelling at the slip of paper I'd been given with the fruits of my occasional bouts of labour printed on it, I shoved the bottle into my handbag and we called a taxi to Fibber's.

Once inside, Anna occasionally nudged me and pointed out a guy she liked the look of, but I was drawn more to the women among the clientele. As it happened, we ran into a girl who had taken to joining us occasionally and she had a friend of hers from Galway in tow. Her pal had short, curly, brown hair, a slim figure and arresting blue eyes. She was the human incarnation of the girl described in that criminally twee 'Galway Girl' track you hear blaring out of Copper Face Jacks every time you walk past. I was instantly attracted to her and my heart did a summersault as she leaned in to kiss me on the cheek when were introduced.

We grabbed a table together and took turns going to the bar for rounds of Diet Coke. It became increasingly difficult to order with a straight face and we would run giggling back to our seats where we would mix in our own vodka. We were hammered by midnight, and the Galway Girl and I were hitting it off. The conversation turned to sex, and she mentioned she was bisexual.

'Have you ever been with a girl?' she asked me with a coquettish smile.

'I kissed a girl once, but that's been pretty much it,' I answered, feeling my cheeks burn slightly.

'You should give it a try,' she said, leaning in to kiss me.

I closed my eyes and tilted my head, while the two other girls whooped and cheered. Her lips were smooth and soft, and tasted of cherry lip-balm and vodka. I'm not sure how long we kissed for, but my head was swimming when we stopped. It was different from the first time I had kissed a girl – that had been nice, but it felt like we had done it for the laugh and for the reaction we might get. This was just the start of something; it felt like foreplay.

She rested her hand on mine, and gave me a lazy smile. I couldn't wait to get out of there. She didn't make me wait long. She leaned in and whispered, 'Your place?' in my ear, out of range of the other two. It was what I had been waiting to hear all night. Without saying a word, I stood up, picked up my bag and led her outside by the hand.

Her hands were all over me in the taxi on the way to my place, and the taxi driver struggled to keep his eyes on the road. By the time we got through my bedroom door we had already pulled off most of each other's clothes.

My memories of the sex are blurred by the amount of drink I put away that night. What I do recall of the experience is in random clips and flashes. I remember going down on her, and not getting it quite right at first. I'd never done it before and I had imagined it to be similar to going down on a guy in terms of speed and pressure. She ran her fingers through my hair slowly and gently, which I took as a cue to be a little less rough. It worked, and she was soon cumming in hard, shuddering bursts.

I woke up the next morning feeling bitterly hungover and painfully awkward about what we had done the night before. I was suddenly acutely aware of the fact that I hadn't a clue what my bed partner's name was. Galway Girl was still sleeping beside me, but the only thing I could think about was how I was going to extricate myself from the situation. I felt like a guy who brings home a chick and then struggles to get rid of her the next morning. She woke up shortly afterwards, arching her back in a slow, feline stretch. I had seen my own reaction in the behaviour of some of the guys I had been with, and I didn't know how to act. Was I the guy in this scenario? Is that how it works? I didn't know what to say ... so I asked if she wanted breakfast. 'Sure,' she said, looking slightly amused by my discomfort.

We went downstairs to eat, me feeling uncomfortable and she largely oblivious. How long was she going to stay? I was busy devising a strategy for hurrying breakfast along when the universe threw me a life ring. There was a knock at the door. We had arranged to get cable TV installed that day. My hangover made me resent how bright-eyed and bushy-tailed the man from NTL looked, but I was still delighted to see him. I kept chatting about access points and charges for service in additional rooms until Galway Girl decided she was surplus to requirements. Within minutes she had pecked me on the cheek and disappeared out the door.

I spent weeks afterwards wondering whether I was in fact a lesbian. I managed to dismiss the idea by reminding myself of the fact that I always had, and still did, love being with guys. I had heard that girls go through phases of being drawn to other girls, and I thought this might explain it. It could have been a curiosity thing. Or maybe I was bisexual. This concept began to gather traction and I decided, while on a visit to Kilkenny, that I should come out to my ma.

'I'm bisexual,' I said, with a solemn look.

'Don't be silly,' she snapped back. 'You can't do that!'

I was stunned.

'Be either straight or gay. Bisexual is just another word for greedy.'

The two of us erupted into a fit laughter.

'I'll put the kettle on,' she said. 'Bisexual my arse.'

Chapter Nine

With my studies firmly behind me, I managed to get another, slightly better-paid job working in a car rental firm at Dublin Airport. I moved into an apartment with a guy I met shortly before my exams. Joseph was a complete stoner and we first got chatting over a shared joint when he asked me for a light when I was on my way to Fibber's. It turned out he was going there too. He was a relaxed, contented chap who was happy in his own skin. I went back to his place on the night we met, and although we had sex, it was immediately obvious that we were not compatible in that department. But even though there was no spark in the bedroom, we got on really well. We both liked video games, listened to the same music and he had a dry, sarcastic sense of humour I couldn't get enough of. With school out of the way, I started hanging out and getting stoned with him a lot. It was during the haze of a Sunday afternoon session that the idea of getting a place together came up. It seemed like a good idea when we were wasted, and didn't seem like an awful one when the smoke cleared.

We got a cheap and nasty place near Dorset Street on the north side of Dublin city centre. The rooms were tiny and damp seeped through the walls. Even when you scrubbed the place it still felt grimy, but at the time I didn't care. I was smoking a lot, still drinking and I knew I wasn't there long-term. What did piss me off about the place was that it didn't have any internet. At first I was determined to have it installed immediately, but as the weeks passed I stopped missing it. It wasn't as painful a break as I thought it would be, considering the net had been a central feature of my life since my early teens. But now that I had a busy real-world social life, it no longer seemed as vital as it once did.

I lasted six months as a stoner slob before deciding it was gross. I started looking for another place and eventually found a room in a large apartment closer to the city centre. It was populated by a mixed group of similarly-aged student types. With my living arrangements settled, I was free to focus on partying, getting drunk in Fibber's and going home with the guys I took a shine to.

The idea that my antics might be earning me a bad reputation did occur to me. You could do whatever you wanted with people you met online because none of them could know what else you were getting up to when they weren't around. In the real world, things were a little bit different, especially when you stuck for the most part to the one bar. I didn't like the idea of guys comparing notes about me, so I avoided sleeping with people who knew each other. But while my conquests themselves were kept largely in the dark, there was no hiding my promiscuous habits from my housemates. They noted the traffic that made its way to and from my bedroom. All I could do was try not to let what others thought of me become an issue.

For my part, I never worried about quantity. In the beginning I tried to keep count, but my magic number shot up so fast that I started counting in tens. Then even that became difficult, as more people slipped in and out of my sheets. And it wasn't just guys, either. I had another lesbian experience shortly after Galway Girl, and then another and another. I did manage to keep track of how many women I had been with: eighteen. It was a useful figure to keep to hand: I could point out to overconfident guys that I had probably pulled more girls than they had.

I sometimes resented the fact that I was supposed to be hiding my habits. Guys could brag about the notches on their bedposts, so why couldn't I? I normally got a positive reaction whenever I revealed the rough number of guys, but these conversations tended to be with Fibber's regulars who would nod their head and say they thought it was cool. They may have said something different behind my back, but I just chalked down as hypocrites people who took a negative view of promiscuity. People's heads turn when a good-looking member of the opposite sex walks past. They want to do something beyond looking, but whether it's Catholic guilt, an unwillingness to go against societal norms or fear of being caught and dumped by a partner, most never act on it. So they'll go to the grave having had a handful of sexual partners. Their reputation will be whiter than white but they will have denied themselves the enjoyment they could have had if they had been brave enough to do things they really wanted to.

There were five others crammed into the flat I shared and every one of them was in a relationship. They were friendly but I rarely socialised with any of them. Staying in meant being surrounded by couples being couply, and it got very annoying, very fast. Worse, Anna had decided to go home, so my night-out options were dwindling. It might sound like a case of the green-eyed monster, but my flatmates were actually turning me off the idea of being in a relationship. I noticed some of them didn't seem to particularly like the people they were with, but they were so against the idea of being single that they just put up with the situation. Two of the girls I lived with chopped and changed boyfriends regularly, pulling new guys off the substitutes' bench when the old model got boring. I couldn't bring myself to put up with someone I didn't like just for the sake of it. There was only one thing for it – the net would again have to save me from a life of boredom and obscurity.

This time around, I wasn't interested in romance, dating or niceties – I was after bullshit-free casual sexual relationships with good-looking guys. If it lasted one night, fine. If it stretched to two or three, then great. If anything threatened to tip over into relationship territory, I would be walking away.

I joined a site called *adultfriendfinder.com* and it turned out to be exactly what it sounded like: a hook-up site. I didn't upload a picture at first and had to rely on my description to draw suitors: five foot with long black hair and blue eyes. Somewhat unsurprisingly given the gender split on the website the offers came flooding in. I cherry-picked the interesting, attractive guys and I was soon back to building a group of on-line 'friends'. When I met up with a man from *adultfriendfinder.com* it was implicit that if an attraction existed, we would be having sex. Awkward trips to the cinema and stilted conversations over dinner were out the window. 'Dates' meant being picked up and taken to a guy's place, or maybe to a hotel. If I didn't like him I would make my excuses before things got to that stage. If I was attracted to the guy I would sleep with him.

It started off as a weekend thing, but I quickly upped my numbers. There was no shortage of guys to hook up with, and I found myself really enjoying the time I spent with some of them. I met my favourites regularly while at the same time keeping a look out for new recruits.

Things began to spiral. I was sleeping with far more guys than I ever thought I would, and when I wasn't having sex I was thinking about it. The net was eating up my time again. I spent hours watching porn, checking my messages on *adultfriendfinder.com* and vetting men I liked the look of. If an instant message popped up on my screen from a guy I liked I would drop what I was doing to go and meet him. If my place was quiet enough, I would invite him over.

It stopped being just a weekend thing. Then it stopped being just a night-time thing. I would meet one guy during the day and another at night. I started going to Fibber's much less and internet hook-ups became the centre of both my social life and my sex life.

I was juggling more than a dozen different guys at one point, each of whom I was meeting regularly. I struggled to meet them all as often as they wanted but I had fun trying. I once met and fucked four of them in one day. I remember thinking how crazy it all was. My hobby had spiralled into a full-blown addiction that dominated my waking hours.

I didn't go to any great lengths to conceal the number of guys I was sleeping with. I knew what people thought of girls who did what I was doing and I could imagine the things that must have been said about me behind my back, but I never let it get to me. I would go into defensive mode whenever the subject came up in conversation and argue that if it was okay for guys to sleep with as many girls as they could then it should be no different for girls. But deep down, I knew this was just paper-thin self-justification. I knew I had a problem, but I couldn't do anything about it. And I was having way too much fun to even consider stopping.

The number of men I was sleeping with wasn't the only concern. I was being drawn to the stranger, more extreme suggestions guys were making. I wanted to push myself to try everything and find out what I did and didn't like. I got a message one day from a guy who had a particularly fucked up idea. He was in his early thirties and looked clean-cut and handsome in his photo. After exchanging the bare minimum of pleasantries, he told me about his fantasy. He wanted me to meet him in a pub in the city centre in broad daylight. He would buy a drink and take a seat next to me. Then he would take out his cock and masturbate while I watched. He didn't want to have sex with me. He didn't want to touch me, or for me to touch him. He didn't even want to speak to me. It wasn't something I ever imagined I would enjoy, but the sheer weirdness of the idea made me want to give it a try. The plan was to meet in the city centre during the day so I thought, *What's the worst that can happen?* I wondered about what I would do if we were seen, but he would be the one caught with his pants down, so I could just pretend to be oblivious to the whole thing. I decided to go for it.

A couple of days later, I walked into a well-known pub in Dublin's Temple Bar, bought a drink and took a seat. My man arrived minutes later. He was wearing an ash-grey business suit, his hair neatly gelled back and he smelled of expensive aftershave. He was more attractive in real life than in his pictures. After getting a drink for himself, he took a seat next to me as planned. I knew I wasn't going to be doing anything, but my heart was about ready to burst with excitement when, calm as you like, he unzipped his fly and took out his dick. What the fuck was I doing? What if we were spotted by the staff and the police were called? How could we explain this one away? He wasn't at all nervous, and he stared straight at me while stroking his cock, without the least glimmer of shame. The pub was quiet, but it wasn't empty. There was a group of three or four Spanish students sitting a few yards away and there was an old guy reading a paper at the bar. The barman was standing within spitting distance, although he was engrossed in conversation with a blonde Eastern European lounge girl, who was leaning against the the bar.

The guy was partly concealed by the table we were sitting at, but it would only take the barman or one of the students to look in our direction at the wrong angle for us to be caught. I stared straight ahead while he worked his cock, but I couldn't resist stealing fleeting glances at what he was doing. I was split between staying until the job was done and sprinting out of the pub. I still hadn't said a single solitary word to this guy and here I was engaged with him in the most bizarre, not to mention illegal, sexual encounter I had ever been involved in.

When he was ready to cum, he had the decency to use a wad of toilet paper he whipped from his pocket. I could just about accept being party to someone wanking in public, but leaving a mess for some unfortunate to clean (or, God forbid, sit on) would have been a bridge too far.

When he finished, he took a gulp from his drink and walked straight out of the pub without a word. I sat there stunned for a moment, before deciding I'd better leave too. I had to force back a giggle when I passed the staff on my way out.

A message popped up on my screen that evening from the phantom wanker. He thanked me profusely for meeting him, adding that our sordid rendezvous had gone down exactly as he had hoped it would. We chatted again a few days later and he admitted that he had no interest in intercourse, oral or anything else – he didn't like being touched. Public masturbation was his thing and it was the only way he could get off. I felt sorry for him.

Although I had a fairly liberal policy regarding who I slept with, I did stick to one rule – I wouldn't hook up with someone, even if they looked amazing, if I didn't get on with them. I would spend weeks establishing what sort of person a guy was before committing to that first meeting. If I liked him and we were compatible in bed, then a repeat performance would always be on the cards. That said, the sheer volume of messages I would get (with accompanying photographs), meant I was able to cherry-pick the lookers.

The result of my screening process was that I often met men who were both strikingly handsome and easy to get on with. Even still, I never got close to any of them. It wasn't what I wanted so regardless of how they felt about it, these relationships were never going to develop beyond the occasional hook-up. I tossed aside all the emotional baggage and I was free to enjoy the physical side of lots and lots of great sex. But as the guys came and went, I occasionally felt like something was missing. In my darker moments, I wondered about whether the couples I derided might have the right idea.

I had got to the point where I hardly differentiated between spending an afternoon playing video games with a guy over a joint and fucking him for the first time. Both had become nothing more than fun things you do with someone you like to hang out with. I wondered if there was something wrong with me. I felt almost inhuman, the way I could completely detach myself emotionally from sex. I thought, *How can you have sex with so many people, but not feel anything with any of them? Surely someone should have triggered something in me by now?* But I just felt nothing other than the physical. I had flicked a switch. When the day came and I wanted to be in a relationship again, would I be able to develop any kind of feeling or attachment? When these thoughts crept in, I would do my best to push them down and plough on. Sex with another drop-dead-gorgeous guy who knew exactly what he wanted in the bedroom would take my mind off the bigger questions.

Chapter Ten

 oing from casually meeting guys on the net to full-on swingers' parties looks a big jump when I think back now, but at the time it felt like a natural progression. The one-on-one sex was often great, but it was becoming increasingly obvious that I was an exhibitionist at heart. The attention I had received when stripping on webcam every other night must have left its mark: I loved being watched.

For weeks I mulled over the idea of getting involved in swinging before finally deciding to log on to a swingers' website, just to see. As usual, there were far more lads than girls floating around, and even the beautiful men clamoured for female attention. The number of men sending me messages skyrocketed when I started stripping on camera in the swingers' site chatroom, just like I had done years earlier. There were other girls who did the same (I could click on their cams and watch) but most were too afraid to show their faces. This wasn't a problem for me; I had done it before and I was still able to walk the streets without being arrested or stoned to death. I didn't care all that much about what people thought or who found out, so I couldn't see any reason to conceal who I was.

As well as swingers' parties and gangbangs, site members used its forum to arrange one-on-one hook-ups. Obviously, this wasn't anything I hadn't done before either, so I decided it would be a good way to ease myself into the scene. The first guy I met from the site picked me up in Dublin and drove me to his place in the country, somewhere in rural Meath. He was good looking – tall, with dark hair and dark eyes – so I wasn't particularly shocked when it came to light that he had a girlfriend. Her picture was sitting on a shelf in the sitting room. *Fuck it*, I thought. It was his problem, not mine.

We were getting down to it in the sitting room within minutes, and when I noticed his laptop sitting beside the sofa I had an idea. I told him to log on to the swingers' website and click on his webcam. I wanted people to see us. He was willing to give it a go, as long as nobody could see his face, so we angled the camera in a way that left his head out of shot. Messages started to fly up on the screen, dozens at first, and then hundreds. I lapped up the attention. I enjoyed it more than the sex.

A site regular who had seen our antics got in touch a few days later. Peter was overweight, in his forties and there was no chance I would consider sleeping with him. But he was a friendly chap and I was happy enough to chat with him. He had been swinging for years and he knew the scene inside out. He was familiar with the goings on on the site and the characters involved, so he was a useful guy to know. He pointed out people he thought I might be interested in, and warned me off the wierdos, who were not in short supply. After a couple of weeks, he mentioned a swingers' party set to take place in Wexford. He planned to go, as did dozens of others from the site. The hosts were a swinging couple who regularly held parties in their big country house. Peter offered to take me.

I had been reading and chatting about swinging for months by then, and I was keen to at least see what the fuss was about. I told Peter I would go, but on the understanding that I wouldn't be doing anything either with him or anyone else who showed up. When the big day came, I took a train to Gorey, where Peter picked me up in his car. On reflection this was another in the long list of unforgivably dangerous things I did, but at the time I didn't take the risks even remotely seriously. The host couple greeted us at the door and invited us in. They were old and fat, borderline obese in fact. They looked like a typical rural couple who didn't get out much and instead sat at home eating and drinking too much. The stereotype was rounded off nicely by almost impenetrable rural Wexford accents.

Peter and I were the first to arrive, and the couple was putting the finishing touches to the spread they were laying out for their guests in the front room. It was like being at a birthday party and there was no sense that anything other than drinks and chit-chat was going to go down. The couple had an interesting dynamic going on – she swung, but he didn't. I first assumed that he must have got off by watching her have sex, but he didn't. He didn't like to be in the same room when she was having sex. He just helped make the sandwiches for the people who came by to fuck his wife.

When I agreed to go I knew to expect some out-there stuff, so I tried to be as open minded as I could. But it was difficult not to get a bit freaked out. There was something surreal about what was going on: polite conversation, compliments on the sausage rolls and zero discussion of the one thing that had brought everyone there.

More people arrived, in ones and twos. With the crowd building, I started to feel a bit out of place. Everyone seemed to already know each other; they had probably done all manner of filthy things to each other. But bar Peter, who I had met an hour beforehand, they were all new to me. Peter must have picked up on my discomfort. He introduced me to the party-goers he was friendly with and tried to include me when he could.

Over twenty people had turned up by nightfall and I was easily the youngest person there. Everyone was in good form, excited about the evening ahead, and they chatted, ate and drank away merrily. The only thing I spotted during those early hours that suggested that the get-together might be anything other than a common-or-garden house party was that the doors of all the rooms upstairs had been left open, and inflatable mattresses had been placed on the floor beside each bed.

I had a few drinks and started to enjoy myself. The atmosphere was cheerful and there was nothing threatening about the vibe. I got no sense of anything predatory or manipulative going on, which to some degree surprised me. Everyone was being very adult. They had all come with an agenda, but it was a shared agenda: to have kinky group sex with strangers and casual acquaintances. It was fun, but I would be sticking to my plan of not having sex. There just wasn't anyone close enough to my age, or whom I found attractive.

Downstairs the normal, birthday-type party continued as it had done, but I noticed the crowd had thinned out. I decided to investigate. I didn't have to search for long, as I could hear noises from upstairs as soon as I walked into the hall. I felt strange about creeping upstairs and into a bedroom occupied by people having sex, even if that was exactly the type of thing they were into, but curiosity got the better of me.

I felt like a giddy kid as I walked gingerly upstairs. The door to the spare room was wide open, the light was on and I had a clear view of what was happening. My eyes nearly fell out of my head. The female owner of the house, now wearing an over-sized yet still too-small corset and suspenders combo, was bent over the side of the bed while being fucked from behind by a hairy-backed party-goer. At the same time, she was going down on a woman who was lying spread-eagled on the bed in front of her. There was a man standing over the second woman, with his cock out. He smiled at me as he dangled his dick into her mouth from above.

I raised my hand to my face in an attempt to conceal a body-shaking fit of giggles. The heads of the entangled foursome swung around to face me and I managed to supress the urge to laugh out loud. They didn't seem too bothered. After a round of smiles and nods of acknowledgement they quickly turned their attentions back to whatever they had been pounding, licking or sucking before I interrupted them.

I went back downstairs to grab a drink only to discover that the polite house-party had been replaced by a wild orgy. It was a sea of wrinkled knobs, saggy tits and wheezing, reddened faces. There were naked old people fucking each other everywhere I looked.

My initial shock dissipated and I remember feeling quite happy with myself for coming to see this bizarre world up close. I was watching something most people will never have any knowledge of. Probably because they wouldn't want to, but still …

Another surprise was the swingers' stamina. They fucked furiously for hours on end. I got the definite impression that the guys were being helped in their sweaty endeavours by some form of medication, but the women were sticking the pace. Some were taking on three, four, five guys one after another without a pause for breath.

As interesting as it was, it didn't turn me on. There

wasn't anyone I was attracted to. There was one guy who was a bit younger than the rest. He was quite good looking and had a smattering of sexy tattoos. I mulled over the idea of approaching him, maybe dropping in front of him and putting his cock in my mouth, but in the end I decided against it. He had a sort of creepiness to him that was a major turn-off, so I went back to giggling to myself at the otherworldly show playing itself out in front of me.

As the drink flowed, I stopped settling for furtive, embarrassed glances of the action and started to stare unabashed at the increasingly wild goings on. I started to feel like a wildlife photographer, looking with a detached curiosity at the mating rituals of a troop of Barbary apes.

It was late by the time libidos and stamina waned, but guests eventually started to drift off for a shower or to crash out on the beds. I grabbed a blanket from the ever helpful male homeowner: the only person besides me to remain clothed throughout, and crashed on the sofa. There were a lot of things going bump in the night, but the half-dozen vodkas I'd drunk helped me off to sleep.

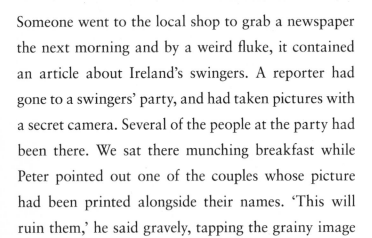

Someone went to the local shop to grab a newspaper the next morning and by a weird fluke, it contained an article about Ireland's swingers. A reporter had gone to a swingers' party, and had taken pictures with a secret camera. Several of the people at the party had been there. We sat there munching breakfast while Peter pointed out one of the couples whose picture had been printed alongside their names. 'This will ruin them,' he said gravely, tapping the grainy image of the pair.

It was sad really. They were a kinky shower, but they seemed pretty harmless. The things they did all took place behind closed doors, so I couldn't see any reason why their privacy should be invaded in such a way, especially when the consequences it would have on their lives and the lives of their families were so serious. I could see why the media would take an interest, but the least they could do was blur faces and not print names.

The assembled group spent some time attempting to pinpoint who the undercover journalist was. After some debate, they singled out a never-before-seen attractive female twenty-something who had turned up on the night. 'It had to have been her,' said Peter with a solemn nod. 'She was far too good looking to be at that party.'

Some of the other party-goers shot glances in my direction. I felt my cheeks burn at what was both a compliment and an accusation.

My ma lived in the middle of the countryside halfway between the party venue and Dublin, so I asked Peter if he could drop me off at her place. No buses went anywhere near her house so she was curious about how in the name of God I'd managed to land myself on her doorstep. I've never had any trouble talking to my ma. She was always open-minded so I didn't see any reason to lie to her. I sat her down and very calmly told her the truth about where I had been.

I had turned twenty-one and I felt I should be able to be honest about these things and have a mature conversation about my sex life rather than hiding it. My ma was considerably less shocked than I thought she would be. In fact, I was the one who was left stunned by the direction the conversation took. Once I'd announced my show-stopping news, she exhaled deeply, smiled and then hit me with it: she'd been to a swingers' party too, and not just as a spectator.

I was dumbfounded. Here I was thinking I was the wild, sexually-liberated free-spirit and I was being comprehensively trumped by my mild-mannered fifty-something mother. I sat there slack-jawed while she calmly explained how she'd gone along to a party back in the 1980s with a female friend of hers. Both of them dived right in, but while her friend went on to become a committed swinger who remained up to her neck in the scene for years, my ma only attended the one party.

She admitted that she had enjoyed the party to some degree, but she said she felt it just wasn't for her. She also had some advice for me: if I couldn't bring myself to get involved in a swingers' party without drinking first, then it wasn't for me either and I should walk away from it. She knew what she was talking about and it was good advice. I didn't listen to her, of course.

Observing at close quarters the sexual practices of old people, topped off with a startling account of my own mother's sex life, made for probably the strangest twenty-four-hour period of my life. It was an eye-opener in a lot of ways, and once I'd calmed down it fed my curiosity. The problem was that there was no way I was going to get down and dirty with the type of forty- and fifty-somethings who populated the Wexford party. There had to be more to the scene than these friendly, adventurous but ultimately unattractive people. I couldn't be the only person in Ireland under thirty with a high sex drive, a lack of interest in a relationship and a willingness to try fucked-up new things.

I remember the exact moment I made the decision to become a swinger. It was Christmas and I was staying at my ma's for the week. I was bored, and something just clicked. I was supposedly in the prime of my life. These were supposed to be the most carefree, thrilling and memorable years I would have. Instead I was bored, lonely and sexually frustrated. This wasn't the life I wanted. I was still battling with the remnants of my teenage self-confidence issues, but I wasn't going to let shyness hold me back.

I came to a decision: I was going to go for it. I was fascinated by swinging and I ached to give it a try, so why shouldn't I? I wasn't going to be the type of person who gets frightened off the things they want to do by what other people might think. My ma already knew I was interested in swinging and she didn't judge me for it. Why should I give a crap what anyone else thought? I knew my dad wouldn't be impressed if he found out, but he was familiar enough with my antics to at least not be very surprised.

I was still just twenty-one, but I'd seen enough of the world to know that people's public personas often bare no relation to the type of person they are behind closed doors. Take John the garda for example. When this upstanding protector of the community wasn't out keeping us all safe, he liked to attempt throat surgery with the end of his cock on underage girls.

The Irish are not known for being the most sexually liberated nation on the planet but the puritan attitude many adopt stinks of hypocrisy. It always seems to be those who thump the pulpit hardest, people who present themselves as whiter than white, who have the dirtiest secrets. The type of people chomping at the bit to judge swingers probably google 'group sex' whenever they're left alone for five minutes with a computer.

I got back from my ma's and logged onto the swingers' site. Messages from young, good-looking, well-turned-out couples, guys and even girls had been accumulating in my inbox.

Simon collected me in the city centre, and we went straight to his place. We had met on the swingers' site and we both knew what we were there for. We were pulling each other's clothes off before his apartment door had closed behind us and we were both naked by the time we reached his bed. I shoved him onto his back, licked my way down his chest and stomach and started sucking. He gripped a handful of hair in each hand and started working his cock in and out of my mouth. I was getting good at giving head: I could take his whole dick into my throat without gagging, gasping or even feeling uncomfortable. He moaned with pleasure as I cupped his balls with one hand and dug my nails into his ass cheek with the other. I was getting wet at the thought of how much pleasure I was able to give him. I loved this subservient role – it gave me a lot more control than I imagined it would.

He hauled me up and flipped me onto my back. He was a big, muscular guy and he loomed large over me when he climbed on top. It might have been intimidating if I didn't want him to fuck me so badly. He didn't require any convincing. We spent the following hours thrashing our bodies against each other before finally collapsing in a sweaty heap on his crumpled sheets. Tender but tingling all over, I was asleep within minutes.

I was curious about Simon. He was a swinger and had been to a bunch of parties. I suppose it showed, as he was lethal in the bedroom. I brought up the subject when we woke the next morning. He said that these days, there was only one party he went to regularly. While most were full of older people with little by way of quality control involved, he had found one get-together that was a little different. It was run by a woman called Angelina who held it at least every couple of weeks. Simon explained that she was around thirty, originally from the Middle East and that she had been organising parties for months. He said they were head and shoulders above anything else he had been to. They were packed with much-better-looking people, most in their twenties or early thirties and there were no weirdos floating around.

The parties were exclusive affairs. Angelina insisted on meeting and vetting beforehand everyone who wanted to go along. If they were normal, stable individuals who otherwise fit the profile of the people she wanted at her parties then they got their first invite. I could handle that. It sounded perfect.

'You should come to one,' said Simon. 'It would be fun to have you there.' He gave me Angelina's number and told me to get in touch. He would give her a call ahead of time to vouch for me.

I wanted to call Angelina that day, but I forced myself to leave it until after Simon cleared it. Three days of phone-checking later, he finally got back to me. He told me he had spoken to Angelina and that she was expecting a call from me. My hands sweated, butterflies fluttered in my stomach and I couldn't wipe the smile off my face. I was really going to do this.

I was a little freaked out that I might say something that would cause Angelina to cast me into the weirdo rubbish basket, so I thought it best to avoid appearing too eager. Nerve-induced procrastination might have had something to do with it, too, because the next day I had to practically force myself to pick up the phone.

When I finally worked up the nerve to make the call, I was immediately put at ease by how friendly Angelina was. She explained that Simon had been singing my praises the previous day. Then, she surprised me. 'I've seen you before,' she said. 'I've seen the shows you've put on online.' After I got over the shock caused by the fact that she had seen me naked, it made sense. We both spent our time in the same online haunts.

'So would you like to meet for a coffee?' she asked.

'Sure,' I said, a surge of bliss bolting up my spine.

It was like being asked out by a guy I'd fallen for. We arranged a daytime meeting in a hotel bar for the following week, and in the meantime we chatted regularly online. We hit it off and by the time the big day came, it already felt like we were becoming friends.

Angelina was sitting at a table in the far corner of the darkened bar with another woman when I arrived. Angelina was petite with dark, shoulder-length hair. She had big, almond-shaped eyes that glistened with intelligence. She looked about thirty and was strikingly beautiful. She had a kind of calm femininity about her that added to her attractiveness.

The girl she was sitting with, Julie, couldn't have been more different in appearance. Julie was a friend of Angelina's whom she had met through swinging. She was over the six foot mark with big, curly blonde hair and a gigantic rack.

I took a seat and Angelina and I were soon chatting like old friends. Julie was nice, but she was less amiable. If someone told me she worked as a bouncer I could easily have believed it. She was a stern, serious individual, someone you wouldn't want to mess with.

I wondered if Angelina brought her along to these meetings in case she ended up with an oddball who turned nasty. If so, she chose well.

I knew by then that swinging attracted all sorts, but Julie didn't strike me as the type. She was outgoing, but in a slightly domineering way. I suppose some guys like that.

Angelina told me a bit about herself, too. Her dad was from the Middle East and her mam was Irish. She had spent her early life in her father's home country before moving to Ireland when she was a teenager.

She was brought up in a strict Muslim household. Her father was hard on her and she was delighted to get away from the life she had. The sense of liberation she felt had carried her first into the sinful West and then all the way into swinging. She had completely turned away from her old life and religion and she hadn't spoken to her father in years.

She met and got married to an Irishman, but they had since separated. He never had any knowledge of her swinging; she turned to it when their relationship was breaking down. She was given an invite by a friend who was involved in the scene and, newly free and single, she decided to go for it. She loved it immediately and was soon going to parties whenever she could. But while some were a lot of fun, she was dismayed by how messy others could get. There would sometimes be too many unattractive people, or the occasional odd character mooching around and making others feel uncomfortable. So she decided to do something about it. She had been organising parties for a couple of months when we met. Simon was one of her first recruits.

Before I left, Angelina asked if I would like to come to what she described as a meet-and-greet. It was a term I was familiar with from the sites. It was a type of pre-sex-party get-together, where would-be and experienced swingers checked each other out, got to know each other and basically decided whether there was any attraction worth pursuing. The swingers' site itself was organising the get-together, and Angelina was bringing along her circle of 'friends'.

It was pretty much all I could think about for the entire week. It didn't help that every time I logged on to the swingers' site, it was practically the only topic anyone spoke about. Dozens mentioned that they were going, and many others were scratching around for invites. It was strictly single girls and couples only, which left single guys out in the cold. Like most of the other girls on the site, I received a ton of messages from guys asking me to the party. Simon couldn't make it and I didn't fancy being someone's entry pass, so I decided to go with a guy I had hooked up with a couple of times before.

I met Eoin through the swingers' site, but he had never gone as far as going to a party himself. He was my age and he was a really nice guy. The first time we met, he booked a hotel room and after a couple of drinks we put it to use. He was eager to make this meet-and-greet his first swinging experience, although he seemed slightly nervous about the whole thing. He decided to book a room in the hotel where the event was taking place. I couldn't help but wonder who we would end up sharing it with.

The excitement built as the party approached. I suppose I was a little nervous too, but I was more excited than anything else. I was like kid at Christmas.

The party was booked for a Saturday, and I remember counting down the days like I was heading off for a week in the sun. Then, the day before, I received a private message from the event organisers. Because it was being put together by the swingers' website, a pair of site moderators, swingers themselves, were handling the logistics. They had booked a downstairs function room in the hotel under the non-specific and somewhat mysterious guise of a Hatter's Tea Party. When I arrived at reception, this was what I should ask to be directed to. They had even arranged for food and a full private bar to be put on by the hotel staff. The message pointed out that everyone was to be on their best behaviour while in the function room, so as not to give the game away. Beyond that, people could book their own rooms and take whoever they wanted back to them. It was all very slick. I was impressed.

I painstakingly chose an outfit, fixed my hair and fussed over my make-up. When Eoin arrived to pick me up I was a little anxious, but I started to feel better when I noticed he was more freaked out than I was. But even as we were pulling up outside, I still hadn't decided how far I was going to go with this. The meeting was officially a meet-and-greet at which nothing would necessarily happen, but there were bound to be some side-celebrations on the go once drink flowed and attraction sparked. I hadn't yet decided to dive straight in, but I wasn't ruling anything out either. It was nearly a year since I had first got interested in swinging. I'd been to one party, but that had been purely as a spectator. This felt like it was going to be different.

The function room was big – and it needed to be. When I shoved open the door there were already a good fifty people standing around inside, nervously sipping drinks in small groups of twos and threes. The first thing I noticed was that the age range was a lot more varied than it had been at the last event I went to. This time it wasn't wall-to-wall old people. Still, at twenty-one, I looked to be the youngest girl present. I didn't mind so much; there were quite a few good-looking guys close to my age in the bunch.

There was a distinct cattle-mart moment when the

door banged shut behind us. Heads turned to see who the latest addition to the party was. I knew I was being appraised by those fifty sets of eyes, but it didn't bother me. I quite liked it.

Everyone had put a lot of effort into their appearance for this one, which was fair enough considering we were all on show. The party-goers were all done up to the nines, with some looking as if they were ready for a job interview. The atmosphere was strange, a little cooler than the last party, but I had expected the initial stilted awkwardness this time around. I knew it wouldn't be long before it faded.

I remember recognising one or two faces in the crowd from their profile photos on the swingers' site, but I got the immediate impression that still more recognised me. I was the youngest girl in the room, and I think I compared well with the other ladies who had turned up. But my age and looks couldn't account for the sheer volume of stares and smiles that came my way.

Then it dawned on me: the room was filled with the people who had been clicking 'view' when I turned on my webcam. Being more exhibitionist than voyeur,

I was never all that interested in seeing what they were up to, so they remained faceless to me. But they were more than familiar with what I looked like. These people had seen me naked, they had seen me playing with myself and if they happened to have tuned in at the right time, they would have seen me have sex on cam. It was bizarre. The anonymous eighty, ninety, one hundred number that appeared next to 'now viewing your cam' suddenly stopped being just a digit and became a room full of people.

I wasn't imaging things; they did recognise me. People started introducing themselves even before I had the chance to grab a drink. They all had nice things to say, although whatever compliment they offered tended to be delivered with a filthy smile. Not that this was a problem. I had spent most of my life hovering around the edges and now I was the centre of attention. I was the main attraction and everyone knew who I was. It wasn't something I was used to, but I was enjoying myself.

A steady stream of people kept coming up to say hello and to tell me they knew who I was. It was guys mostly, but girls too. Some went as far as to casually mention that they had booked a room upstairs. I was more than welcome to drop by for a drink when things wound down in the function room, they said. Sure, it would have been nice to have been known for something other than being the girl who gets down and dirty on her webcam, but I didn't really care. I just liked the fact that they were competing for my attention.

Just like every other party, swing or otherwise, everyone started to loosen up as the night closed in and the drink flowed. It was good craic. People started milling around and talking to each other rather than sticking rigidly to the small groups of two or three they had arrived in.

Eoin, however, didn't seem to be enjoying himself. He seemed a bit overwhelmed and was reluctant to mingle. Instead he went back and forth from the bar, gulping down pints in the hope that alcohol might wipe out his anxiety. He invariably returned with a drink for me too, and it wasn't long before I was feeling the effects.

He insisted on paying for everything and this made me feel for the guy. I started to reflect on our relationship to date. He was a lovely chap but he had been behaving strangely of late. I enjoyed hanging out with him as well as the sex, but I had absolutely no intention of getting into anything serious with him. I had thought he was on the same page, but it was starting to look a bit like he was angling for something more. We had slept together a handful of times, but he had been suggesting the cinema, meals and various other date-like scenarios of late. Things couldn't continue like this.

I didn't want to just ditch him in the middle of the party, but I needed to make sure that it was clear to him, as well as to everyone else, that we were not an item. It was a strange thing to have to consider at an event like that, I thought. The added benefit of putting a sliver of distance between Eoin and me was that it meant I could chat more freely with the other swingers. Being the girl in the room everyone wanted to know felt good. It was an ego boost and I could feel it charging my confidence. I wanted to lap up the experience.

Although I had come to the party thinking that there was a good chance I wouldn't do anything and that it was a social gathering first and foremost, I soon changed my mind. I wasn't going to be able to help myself from getting involved. The excitement was getting to me and I knew it was bound to happen.

I caught sight of Angelina shortly after I arrived, and we gradually worked our way across the room towards each other. She was her normal friendly self, but she had a glint in her eye and a sly smile that I hadn't seen the first time we met. This was Angelina in her element. The conversation flowed between the two of us and it started to feel like she was flirting with me. Her jet-black eyes gazed into mine as we chatted while her delicate hands alternated between stroking the stem of her wine glass and touching me gently on the arm.

She was squeezed into a tight black dress that revealed a shapely pair of legs and a hint of cleavage. As we spoke, I found my interest being drawn into her exotic looks and calm, confident demeanour. Although understated at first, when you looked at this girl – really looked at her – her sex appeal became almost overpowering.

'So,' she said, letting the word roll off her tongue, 'where are you sleeping tonight?'

'My plans haven't progressed very far beyond staying with my date,' I said, nodding towards Eoin who was still engrossed in his attempt to drain the bar of its contents.

'I've got an idea,' said Angelina with a look that bordered on the obscene.

'Go on,' I said, incapable of concealing the smile that cut unexpectedly across my face.

'Let's make someone's night.'

As it turned out, she had someone in mind. She told me about how she had been chatting online with a fireman, adding that he was as good looking as he sounded.

'Where is he?' I asked.

Angelina nodded conspiratorially towards a tall, dark-haired thirty-something who was speaking to a couple close to the bar. He was wearing a white shirt that gave away the cut body beneath. The jury is still out on whether or not what they say about firemen is true, but this one made my legs go weak. I looked back to Angelina who was giggling at my reaction.

'Go and keep your date company for a while,' she said with a faux-serious expression. 'Try and make him feel better about the fact that he'll have to do without you for the night.' With that, she walked towards the fireman who, when he saw her approach, immediately disengaged from the conversation he was having. She had turned my head, too. Angelina and the fireman were the two best-looking people in the room and there was no doubting this girl's ability to snare our man. I wouldn't be able to resist an offer of a night with those two.

At some point during the festivities, Eoin came to tell me he was going to bed. He hesitated for a moment, clearly hoping, despite the mounting evidence to the contrary, that I would come with him. This groundless optimism, built on what appeared to be an expectation that I would feel guilty enough about him paying for my company (and not really getting it) to sleep with him, was almost enough to make me stop feeling sorry for the guy. Happily, when I gave him a distinctly friend-like kiss on the cheek, he spared me any type of scene and headed timidly towards the exit.

I met a lot of people that night but after hearing Angelina outline her plans for the evening, every other conversation seemed innocent. There were plenty of other good-looking people at the party and some of the offers I heard were interesting, but there was only one after-party I wanted to be at. With Eoin safely tucked up in bed, most likely alternating between bouts of crying and masturbation, I decided to re-join Angelina. She had spent much of her night chatting with an extremely-pleased-with-himself fireman. He beamed a gorgeous smile at me as I walked towards them. Angelina had obviously already shared her plan with him.

I managed to slip quite seamlessly into their conversation, which revolved around, for the most part, checking out the other people in the room. Because I knew practically no one there, they filled me in on some of the people I should get to know if the opportunity arose, as well as some people I should avoid.

From his body language, it was obvious that the fireman was smitten with Angelina. That said, the way he looked at me suggested he wouldn't object to a third wheel. The subtle, lingering gazes and little touches that the three of us exchanged were discreet at first, but they quickly escalated and we were soon flirting outrageously with each other. The sexual tension was electric – it crackled and snapped with every slow smile and re-crossing of legs.

At one point, Angelina's attention was drawn to a small, cute, blonde girl who had arrived late. She appeared to be joined at the hip to the guy she came with. But while he was scanning the room like a nervous meerkat, she seemed to be enjoying herself. For a start she kept smiling in our direction. It wasn't hard to see why he was feeling a little protective of her. With her big, Bambi-like brown eyes and a petite, curvy frame, she was stunning.

'Why don't you go and speak to her?' said Angelina, revealing her now trademark sly, sexy smile. I was hesitant at first, but since Angelina had done all of the recruiting so far that night I decided I'd better chip in.

'I can do that,' I said, feeling flushed with the confidence garnered from being approached, complimented, and pursued more in the previous three hours than I had in my entire life to that point.

'Tell her we'll probably be turning in soon,' Angelina added. 'See if she wants to join us.'

It was a cheeky assumption, but not one I was about to argue with.

Just as I started to walk towards them, the male half of the duo walked off towards the bathroom, leaving his partner alone. As I got closer, it became clear that my initial from-a-distance impression was right – she was beautiful, and she was interested.

'Hi,' I said, wondering how in the name of God I was going to go about asking this person I had never spoken to in my life if she wanted to have sex with me and some friends I had just made. 'I'm Katie.'

'I recognise you,' she said with a grin, moving in to kiss me on the cheek. 'I like your work. I'm Rose.'

'Thanks,' I mumbled, feeling my cheeks flush. 'Have you been to many of these events?'

'This is our second. We haven't actually gotten involved with anyone just yet, though. He's a little bit unsure about the whole thing,' she added, nodding towards the bathroom door her partner had disappeared through.

'And what about you?' I asked.

'Oh, I'm sure.'

Her boyfriend, Thomas, emerged from the bathroom. He looked stern, and not at all like he wanted to be here.

'Okay, I'll leave you to it,' I said. 'But we'll be heading upstairs soon. You two are more than welcome to join us.'

'Hmmm,' said Rose with a filthy smile, looking over my shoulder at Angelina and the fireman before directing her attention back to me. 'I'll see if I can win this guy over. If he's game, I'm game.'

With that, I went back to Angelina and told her how things went. She decided that we'd give it half an hour, and if they didn't approach us by then we would stop by and ask them if they were interested on our way to bed. About twenty minutes later, when I was recharging my glass at the bar, Rose walked up behind me and placed something in my hand before following her boyfriend towards the exit. It was a phone number with an X underneath. I went back to Angelina and the fireman and explained what happened. 'We'll call her later,' said Angelina. 'Let's go to bed.'

With that, she took both me and the fireman by the hand and led us towards the door.

Standing in the lift, I suddenly realised just how much I'd had to drink. Eoin had bought me a considerable amount, as had a rolling cast of other hopefuls. I'd rounded this off with what I had bought myself and the end result was a pretty drunk Katie.

Maybe it was the alcohol, but I wasn't nervous. I felt quite comfortable with the fireman, Angelina and with the rest of the crowd that had turned up to the meet-and-greet. Everyone I had met was really nice. Even if the night had ended without any sex, I would still have enjoyed myself as much as I had at any other party. I couldn't help but wonder if I would have been treated the same if I had been older or if people didn't know who I was. But at the end of the day, I was young, they did know who I was and they all fell over themselves to be around me. I'd had a great night.

By the time we got to the hotel room I had shifted from wondering whether I would get involved to itching to get started. I didn't have to wait long.

Angelina went into the room ahead of me, with the fireman behind us, and she was already undoing the zip at the back of her low-cut dress before the door swung closed behind him. It fell to the floor at her feet revealing a toned, golden-skinned body. Still in her underwear and heels, Angelina stepped over her dress and eased herself onto the king-sized bed. Drink and adrenaline were making my head spin, and it felt like things were moving quickly. I turned around to see a grinning fireman unbuttoning his crisp, white shirt as quickly as he possibly could. I helped him with his belt, and we were soon frantically pulling each other's clothes off and kissing like over-excited teenagers. With our clothes in an unseemly heap on the floor, he put his giant hands around my waist, lifting me clear off the ground and onto the bed next to Angelina. She giggled when I landed, sliding herself between me and the fireman. I closed my eyes, and took in as much of what was happening as I could through the alcohol fog. I remember the sweet, citrus smell of Angelina's perfume and the softness of her lips as she kissed my neck. My breath came in short, sharp bursts as my mind struggled to process the wandering, stroking and caressing of the four hands moving all over me.

I opened my eyes to see Angelina on all fours on the bed with the fireman standing behind her. She stared intently at me while she eased herself back onto his cock. She dipped her head and let out a low groan as he upped the pace and started slamming her. She regained her composure, staring into my eyes again while tracing her nails down my hips. She pulled my legs apart before running her tongue down the inside of my thigh.

I gripped the headboard behind me as she went down on me. This girl knew what she was doing. The fireman looked at me with bad intent while still ramming his cock into Angelina. I stared back at him – partly fearful, partly eager. He picked up the pace, and Angelina wrapped her arms around my thighs and dug in her nails. Her body jerked and thrashed, and she came hard. The fireman was clearly pleased with his handy work. He pulled out, leaving Angelina to collapse in a panting, grinning heap. He snapped off the condom I hadn't notice him put on and grabbed a fresh one from table next to the bed. Once he was rubbered up, I took him by the cock and gently guided him into me. He was big, but I was already wet from Angelina and he pushed his way in easily.

The fireman wasn't in the mood for gentle, romantic love-making. I could tell by the look on his face that he wanted to show that he was more than enough man for the two of us. I remember reading somewhere that every man wants to be a tyrant in the bedroom, and this guy was out to teach us a lesson. He planted his big arms on the bed on either side of me, and I wanted him to take control – I wanted him to be the boss.

The fireman spent the next two hours proudly demonstrating his ridiculous stamina before the three of us collapsed into a sweaty pile on the bed. After catching her breath, Angelina leaned over and picked up a piece of paper that was lying next to my bag. It was the phone number Rose had given me earlier. She grabbed her mobile and punched in the digits. The fireman and I sat there smiling while Angelina chatted with her. As it turned out, her boyfriend had decided he wanted an early night and that she would be having one too. She wasn't happy with how her night had ended and she wanted to try to sneak out to join us. She gave Angelina her room number and suggested one of us come and get her. Both the fireman and Angelina looked at me.

'No problem,' I said, playfully punching Angelina on the arm. 'I'll give you two some privacy.'

Pulling my clothes back on was a major undertaking, and the reality of just how drunk I was really hit home. I staggered out the door and into the hallway, with absolutely no concept of which direction I should go in. I wandered around for what felt like hours, trying to find the right room. When I eventually found it, I knocked gently on the door, fixing my hair and adjusting my clothes as best I could before it swung open. When it did, a small, bald man with a jutting, hairy belly stood squinting suspiciously at me. 'Sorry!' I gasped. 'I've got the wrong room.' He started to mumble something, but I didn't hang around to hear what it was.

After that there was some more aimless wandering in the search of the room I had come from. When I finally found it, I could hear that the fireman had got a second wind. I bleeped the door open and walked inside. The fireman had Angelina on her back at the edge of the bed. Her legs were over his shoulders and he was slamming into her with eye-watering force. I pulled a chair from the corner of the room, dragged it next to the bed and sat down. My feet were killing me; I had spent far too long in uncomfortable shoes. I looked dispassionately from inches away as bursts of ecstasy and pain flashed across Angelina's face. She would occasionally lock eyes with me, moaning as the fireman pushed his cock as far inside her as he could. After a few minutes, the fireman decided it was my turn. He pulled out of Angelina and started undressing me again. 'Didn't I strip you naked already?' he said, a look of mock sternness on his face.

Within seconds, I was lying on the bed next to Angelina with my legs on the fireman's shoulders. The position allowed his dick to go deep – I was practically impaled. I could see why Angelina's expressions were a tad anguished. She moved off the bed and into the chair, and after a few minutes the fireman picked up the pace. He closed his eyes, tilted back his head and I knew he was about to cum. He suddenly pulled out his cock, whipped off his condom and took me by the hair. I knew what he wanted, and I was happy to help the guy out. I opened my mouth and, with a guttural groan, he shot straight into it. I patted him on the arse when he finished and walked into the bathroom to spit out his load. He looked slightly disappointed. Tough shit. I didn't like him that much.

I woke up the next morning with a banging head and a churning stomach, but without even a trace of guilt. My recollection of what had gone on was hazy, and it came back to me bit by bit, but I knew that overall I had enjoyed it. Okay, so I hadn't got involved in an all-out orgy, but I had had sex with two people at the same time, both of whom were certified swingers. I had thought about the idea of getting involved for so long that I had built it up beyond what it really was. As it turned out, it was really easy to do. The sex had been amazing, but I enjoyed the socialising aspect, too. The people I had met were all cool, there was no drama and the party had been fun. I would definitely be doing it again.

The three of us showered and headed downstairs for breakfast. I was met by the sobering sight of Eoin making sad faces at a plate of sausages and eggs. I took a seat opposite him, ruffling his hair as I sat down. I felt a bit bad about how he had been so thoroughly cut out of the loop, but at least he now knew that any feelings he might have been developing for me were entirely misplaced. When I asked him if he was okay, he put his bad mood down to an atrocious hangover. He really was a nice fella – he again spared me a scene. We were soon chatting like nothing out of the ordinary had happened. At the table next to Eoin was a married couple in their mid-thirties whom I recognised as having been at the party.

'Were you around when the trouble kicked off?' the male half asked me.

'What trouble?' I said, with no clue what he was talking about.

As it turned out, the function room next to our Hatter's Tea Party had been rented out by some sort of sales convention and the guys attending it ended up getting absolutely wasted. Somehow, word had got around that they were next door to a swingers' party, and they came into our function room firing abuse at people. Some of the swinger guys had taken objection, and punches flew. It turned into a full-blown drunken horror show and ended with someone getting a bottle smashed over his head.

Other people from our party started trickling down to the breakfast room and soon, over a dozen of us were sitting together, chatting about the night before. Even if the main topic of conversation was the mayhem that had rounded off the night, it was a great way to wind down the party. We were all still in hangover mode, and we joked about some of the other things that had happened the night before. We smiled at the good bits and cringed at the bad.

I finally left three hours later, and then only because Eoin had to get back so he could get ready for work. I dived straight into bed as soon as I got home, but I was too excited to sleep. It had been a wild night, but it would pale in comparison with what was to come.

Chapter Eleven

hings between Eoin and me ground to a halt. He came over to my place a few days after the party and one of my housemates recognised him. Unbeknownst to the both of us, he turned out to be the brother of her best friend. That was the final nail in the coffin. I could handle my housemates knowing that I took guys home but, although I wouldn't exactly be suicidal if they found out about my involvement with swinging, I wanted to keep the two sides of my life separate if I could. So I called Eoin and told him we needed to cool things off. He agreed, maintaining the pretence that he too was just after something casual.

After that, he occasionally texted to ask if I wanted to hang out, but it was obvious that he wasn't after friendship. He didn't seem to care that I had ditched him at the party. I know I would have. He had paid for a room, brought me to and from the hotel and paid for drinks all night. He didn't even try to pull anyone else after it became clear that I wasn't interested. If that had been me, I would have been seriously pissed off, and the fact that he wasn't made it obvious how he felt.

With nice-but-sappy Eoin out of the way, I was back online. Having put faces to usernames at the party, I now had a better idea of who I should and shouldn't chat with. While nearly everyone was pretty cool, I was surprised by how different some of the people turned out to be in real life compared with how they came across on the net. Attending also let people know I was willing to go along to events and get involved. This made me even more desirable to the men. I got one message from a guy I cammed with from time to time who said he was delighted to see I was actually real. He explained that some online users displayed recordings of girls stripping on webcam, sourced from God knows where, and then passed them off as themselves doing their thing live.

I wanted to go to another party. I had a lot of fun at the first one, and I wasn't about to start agonising over whether I should go to a second. Happily, Angelina had an offer for me.

She had a birthday coming up and she wanted to mark it with a swingers' party. This was going to be a more selective affair than the meet-and-greet evening, and she planned to limit the number of guests to fifteen. No expense was spared: she booked a swanky suite in a hotel in West Dublin. As well as two giant king-size beds in separate rooms, there was also a living/dining room with a small kitchen attached. It was all dark wood, flatscreens and crisp white linen. It crossed my mind that money could be made from this racket, but that didn't seem to be Angelina's agenda. She was happy for everyone who came to throw a few euro towards covering costs and leave it at that.

She was in a giddy mood when I arrived, excited about how nice the room was and at the thought of the night ahead. A guy called Nigel from the site had helped her organise the party, and I got the impression that she was developing a bit of a thing for him. She had known him for some time, and his name had come up in conversation before. Nigel was the first to arrive and I was immediately struck by his appearance. He was in his late thirties and was just under six foot. He had light brown hair that was thinning slightly on top, and he had a bit of a belly. He was a very average-looking guy and I initially wondered what Angelina saw in him.

Once we started chatting, however, it soon became obvious what Nigel had in his favour. The guy had the gift of the gab and he had charm in spades. He had a flair for storytelling that was complemented wonderfully by his Northern Irish accent. He was soon rattling off tales of sordid situations he had found himself embroiled in, while Angelina and I sat listening, either wide-eyed or doubled over in tears of laughter. He had this subtle way of talking himself up that was very believable. He gave the impression that he was someone who could talk his way out of, or into, any situation. He came prepared, too. As well as the usual bag of drink he also brought a bottle of expensive champagne, several punnets of strawberries and three cans of whipped cream. 'Don't ask!' he said while unpacking and loading them into the fridge.

The rest of the group started to arrive about an hour later. I had brought my laptop with me, and we entertained ourselves by logging onto the swingers' website and chatting with whoever was online. Angelina knew a lot of people, and only a small number managed to get an invite. It gave me an idea.

Drinks flowed and knocks on the hotel room door started coming with increasing frequency. By 9 p.m. all fifteen people had turned up. There were a couple more guys than girls, although it was pretty even. Angelina introduced me to the ones I hadn't already met as they arrived, and there were some interesting individuals among them. One was a garda. She barely had to mention it; he looked every inch a cop. 'Don't hold it against me,' he said, looking like he was genuinely feeling guilty about the career path he had chosen.

He was a really nice chap and was a regular on the scene. He told me how he had to go to extreme lengths to prevent his night-time activities becoming known.

He had two phones – one for his swinging friends and one for his everyday friends. The man was living two completely separate lives.

While most people arrived in pairs, a petite woman in her early forties, with tanned skin and blonde hair, arrived alone. She was expensively dressed and was clearly a bit of a gym bunny. She looked far younger than her years. She told me later that she was married – and that her husband had no idea she was involved in swinging. She also had the type of unforgiving career that would be destroyed if her sexual habits had ever become known. She was a teacher.

With everyone getting comfortable in each other's company and the party-proper feeling like it was about to kick off, Nigel decided it was time for the 'birthday cake'. He grabbed the strawberries and cans of cream from the fridge before whispering something in Angelina's ear. She pulled away with a look of shock on her face, before playfully slapping him on the arm.

'Everyone,' he shouted at the top of his voice, 'instead of giving Angelina a birthday cake, I decided it might be a better idea to turn her into one.' With that, he cleared everything from the table in the dining room before peeling the clothes off a grinning Angelina.

My laptop was still logged on to the swingers' site, so I held it in the air. 'Anyone mind if we show the world?'

The garda and the teacher stepped aside, but everyone else was happy for me to go ahead. I clicked on my webcam and positioned the laptop so it could capture the action. When Angelina was completely naked, Nigel lifted her off the ground and laid her out on the table. He shook the cans of cream and handed one to me with a theatrical wink. The two of us covered her head to toe in cream while the others decorated her with the strawberries. Once we were finished, a dozen of us surrounded the table and licked it all off. I glanced up at my computer while we were tucking in; it looked fit to crash with the number of messages coming through.

This was the trigger the party needed, and clothes were soon hitting the floor. We clicked off the camera so the two exiles could rejoin the party. Things got very hot, very fast and the beds were put to use within minutes. I kept myself in the heart of the action. I had sex with half a dozen guys that night, as well as a couple of girls. We got drunk together, played with the whipped cream some more and fooled around with the webcam. This was my first time getting fully involved in a swinger's party and it was everything I'd hoped it would be.

As time went by, Angelina and I became good friends. We would hang out together outside of the swing scene, going for a drink or grabbing a coffee. She would talk about the tough time she'd had when her marriage began to break down, and she would sometimes bring up details of her previous life in her home country. Her stories of beatings and repression at the hands of a tyrannical, religion-obsessed father were the stuff of nightmares.

She sometimes invited me round to her house, where she lived with her cute, lively eleven-year-old daughter. I started to spend a lot of time at her place and Angelina sometimes asked me to babysit if she needed to be somewhere. Angelina's daughter was an only child, so she was a little bit spoiled at times. She occasionally played her mother off against her father, but that was probably just her way of coping with their separation. She was a good kid, really.

The chronic boredom I was forced to endure at my job in the airport meant I pulled the occasional sickie. The occasional turned into the frequent, and I was eventually called in and told that I was being let go. I was relieved, to be honest. It also threw up an opportunity. When I told Angelina, she suggested a solution. Angelina worked in IT for a bank, but she had been part-time for years. They eventually offered her a full-time position but this meant she needed to arrange childcare. There was a crèche within minutes of Angelina's house, but her daughter didn't take to it. So, Angelina suggested paying me to look after her. It was as easy as jobs came. All I would need to do was take her to and from school and keep an eye on her in Angelina's place until she returned from work.

In a way I was surprised that she would put someone she had met through swinging in charge of her daughter, but we had become close, so it wasn't as bizarre as it sounds on paper. I decided to give it a try, and I wound up taking care of Angelina's lovely daughter for a whole summer.

With my second party under my belt, I threw myself into the swinging scene with the same reckless enthusiasm I had displayed when I started meeting guys from *adultfriendfinder.com* for one-on-one sex. I had yet to encounter a problem, but I never turned up alone all the same. I never really knew what I was going to find at my next party so it seemed a good idea to have someone there to keep an eye on me. I normally turned up with Angelina, or else I would bring a guy who I had previously met and hooked up with.

I also started helping Angelina to vet people who wanted to join her parties. We swapped photos of the hottest of the candidates who wanted an invite, and decide who we would like to meet. Then we arranged to meet guys, girls and couples in pubs or coffee shops around the city, to see what they were like in person. Afterwards, we decided if we wanted to let them come along. It was a bit like an interview, except rather than offering a job to the successful candidates we invited them to a party and fucked their brains out.

As we got to know each other better, I noticed something about Angelina. She seemed to quite easily get attached to guys she had met through swinging. The swinging scene had to be the worst place in the world to find someone you could form a lasting, healthy relationship with, but she was undeterred. The attention she got from people seemed to trigger something in her, but the vast majority of guys who were involved in swinging weren't interested in anything beyond sex. I can't criticise them for that – that's what I was there for too. I suppose Angelina wasn't quite as good at shutting off her emotions as I was.

I started to wonder about what had prompted her to get involved in swinging in the first place. She gave the stock answer of wanting to have a bit of fun as myself, but I felt there had to be more to it than that. Everyone likes having fun but not everyone becomes a swinger. I think her involvement was prompted by the personal problems she was having. Her marriage had just broken down and she was going through a separation, and I think this had hit her confidence. Swinging was an easy way to get the affection she probably needed at the time. Surrounding yourself with people who lust after you can be very reassuring. But much of the affection you get is just smoke and mirrors thrown up by people attempting to disguise that they're out for what they can get from you. It's fine when you're out for what you can get from them too, but I felt that maybe Angelina was looking for something more.

The situation with her father was probably a factor, too. He was consistently horrible to her for years after she moved to Ireland. Angelina told me about how she had brought her daughter back to the Middle East to meet her family shortly before we met, but her father didn't even want to see her. He didn't want to have anything to do with either of them.

The way her father had treated Angelina all her life might have left her craving male attention. Couple this with her determination to break from the strictness of her upbringing and you can see why she might have gone in the direction she did.

Only Angelina knows the full truth behind why she got involved, but she did seek emotional support from people who were, in reality, looking for something less complicated.

The Irish swingers' website I used had thousands of members and although they were not all frequent visitors, the numbers involved, even going by the hundreds that might be online at any given time, were far beyond what I had expected. And that wasn't the only swinging site on the net catering to the Irish market. Swinging in Ireland wasn't an obscure niche populated by a handful of middle-aged oddballs; this was a massive underground scene. Judging by the number of new couples and singles that appeared on the site every week, it was growing fast. So it was unsurprising that Angelina's parties were far from the only show in town.

Thomas was known for throwing the biggest swingers' parties in Ireland. I would see them mentioned on the website in the run-up to one being held, and the day after they took place the site's forums would be buzzing with chatter from members gossiping about how many people had turned up, and about who did what. Although his get-togethers didn't have the level of exclusivity that Angelina's parties had, the guys and girls I spoke to about them invariably reported having a good time. I decided to give one a try.

Getting an invite was easy. I sent Thomas a message asking if I could come, and how much he was charging. He told me I could come for free. I had recently started chatting with Anad, who came from the Far East and had been working in Dublin for a few years. Anad told me he had been to one of Thomas's parties with his then girlfriend and he was eager to go along to the next one, which was being billed as one of the biggest in Ireland to date. I had been looking for an excuse to meet him, so we decided to go together.

I thought Anad might have been winding me up when he told me he was a surgeon, but when he pulled up outside my house in a brand new black Jaguar S-type, it started to look like he could be telling the truth. I was impressed, and even more so when he told me he had booked a room for the two of us in the Four Seasons for a one-on-one after-party. Anad turned out to be just as friendly, relaxed and easy to talk to in person as he had been online. Even though he was a good fifteen years old than me, he was handsome, funny and had a calmness about him that I instantly liked.

I didn't know the circle of swingers that attended Thomas's parties, so I was glad to have Anad around, especially as he had been to a previous event. Thomas had booked a massive luxury short-term-rental apartment near Temple Bar for the night, and it was already heaving when we arrived. I looked around in disbelief at the number of people there. There must have been between seventy and eighty people. Guys outnumbered girls by around two to one, and although it was only 7.30 p.m., the drink was already flowing.

I could see why Thomas had a reputation for not having much regard for quality control. I had heard that he was willing to extend an invite to any girl who wanted to go and that was backed up by what I saw. At the risk of sounding bitchy, some of the girls were not exactly pin-up material.

It wasn't all bad. There were over forty guys there and even if it was by chance rather than by design, some of them were stunners. There were some interesting couples there, too. I immediately noticed a guy in his forties with what turned out to be a Russian girl in her mid-twenties. She was a bombshell: tall, long blonde hair, blue eyes and immaculately put together. She wore a shimmering cocktail dress with a split running midway up her thigh. It revealed toned, tanned legs that seemed to go on for ever. The guy was Irish, and with his deep tan and tailored shirt and trousers, he looked like he was worth a few quid. It would certainly help to explain how he had managed to get his hands on a girl that good looking.

I noticed too that although I was approaching twenty-two, I was still the youngest girl there. With so many people around, it was easy to feel a bit overwhelmed, so I planned to take my time about getting involved. Anad, for his part, didn't seem to be taking much notice of the other girls at the party.

We had been drinking steadily for nearly two hours when things kicked off. The first to get stuck in was the Russian girl. She was chatting to a couple and a guy at the door to one of the bedrooms, when she suddenly dropped to her knees and started unbuckling the single guy's belt. He looked slightly taken aback, suddenly not at all sure if he wanted to be the only guy in the packed room with his dick out, but he was brave enough to let her continue. When she put his cock in her mouth he was still soft, but not for long. Next, she started groping the crotch of the other guy she had been speaking too, all the while completely ignoring the wealthy-looking chap she had arrived with. This, however, didn't seem to be a problem for him. He stood leaning against the wall sipping on a glass of wine while admiring his girl's work, as she alternated between sucking one cock and the other.

The Russian's decision to dive in acted as a spark and the flame she lit quickly spread to engulf the whole room. Conversations were suddenly abandoned and everyone started getting stuck into each other. Clothes were flying off and dicks were coming out all over the room.

A tall, fair-haired guy with sparkling blue eyes walked up to me and put out his hand to introduce himself. He was so pretty that I couldn't resist him. I slapped his hand away and threw my arms around him, kissing him passionately. It was all the encouragement he needed, and he guided me across the room, down a short corridor and into one of the bedrooms. I snatched a glance at Anad. He was walking quickly after me, carrying our drinks and wearing a broad smile. I sat on the bed, noticing that the bedroom was rapidly filling up with guys who had followed us in. My new blonde-haired friend was busy unbuckling his belt, and I was slightly perturbed to notice that a lot of the other guys in the room were doing the same. The guys kept coming, but they stood around the perimeter of the room rather than trying to get in on the act.

I liked having an audience, but this was pushing it. There were soon nearly thirty guys jammed into the room. It was exciting, but I was getting scared. What if they decided to get pushy about it? What would I do? Anad, who was now barely able to see over the gathering crowd, wouldn't be able to do much either. *Fuck it*, I thought, pulling my new man's dick from his boxers and ramming it straight into my mouth.

My confidence grew as I worked his cock, and I

scanned the room to see what else was on offer. I noticed a stocky guy in his late twenties with a shaved head and a sexy tattoo that ran up the side of his neck. It was just visible from under his shirt. He had an anaesthetising stare, and he carried himself with the self-assured air of a boxer. He noticed me looking at him and he stepped forward, taking out his cock as he walked towards me. I took him in my mouth while wanking off the first guy, who was now busying himself with removing my clothes. After a few minutes, I lay back on the bed while the two of them slid off my trousers and underwear. I felt self-conscious at first, but the drink I had put away at home and during the two-hour get-to-know-you period helped. By the time the tattooed guy had slid on a condom and pushed himself inside me, I had completely stopped caring about the number of eyes boring into me.

The blonde guy positioned himself above me, so I went back to sucking him off while the tattooed boxer went to work. He gripped my hips with his powerful hands and started pounding on me. The muscles in his arms tightened and I felt helpless. He was strong enough to do exactly as he wanted with me – nobody was going to stop him. I looked around to see that see Anad had pushed his way to the front of the crowd, but he didn't seem inclined to get involved. He looked slightly awkward standing there, still holding my drink, but he didn't appear to be bothered by how events were unfolding. He even smiled at me when we caught each other's eye. Behind him I noticed a tall, slim, dark-haired boy in his early twenties. He looked a bit doe-eyed, but he was just so adorable when he approached the bed that I couldn't resist letting him get involved. I was still a little shocked at how fast things were progressing. Less than ten minutes ago, I thought, I was standing with Anad, having a drink in a room packed with fully clothed people. Now, I was attending to three cocks while nearly thirty guys watched from inches away. I should have been petrified, but the danger was an aphrodisiac.

I was almost relieved when I noticed the Russian girl strolling into the room with her partner in tow. I was happy to have someone to share the load with, so to speak. She was completely naked and she walked straight over to the bed and bent over it. A second guy who had walked into the room behind her was fumbling with a condom, panicking at the thought that if he didn't get it on fast enough, he might miss the chance of a lifetime. He managed to get himself sorted before she lost interest and he was soon fucking the blonde from behind like an over-excited rabbit.

Soon afterwards a third girl came into the room. She was a tiny Asian girl who looked Filipina. She had a Dublin accent and she looked to be two or three years older than me, which made her the youngest female I had come across on the swinging scene. She had two guys with her and she was blanking the other guys in the room. She appeared to have a very specific goal in mind as she shoved one of her men onto the bed and climbed on top of him while the crowd looked on open-mouthed. Then, the second guy positioned himself behind her and started fucking her in the ass while the first guy was still inside her. I'd seen this in porn, but I had no idea people actually did it in the real world. She was so small; I had to wonder how she didn't break.

Every so often I felt a hand on my shoulder, when another guy from the group decided to make his move.

It can be difficult for guys – they don't always know how to go about getting involved and there can be logistical problems. Girls are pretty much ready to go whenever they want to, but it's not the same for a man. He has to get hard, and then stay hard while picking the right moment to make his approach. If I liked the look of him and was feeling charitable, I would suck him off for a while or maybe let him inside me. When someone tried to get involved and I wasn't interested I just blanked them or gave a curt 'no thanks'. That room full of horny guys looked an intimidating prospect, especially when I was naked on a bed, having sex with someone I didn't know, but they were all remarkably well behaved. Anytime I gave the brush-off, the disappointed guy would just move on without complaining.

With six or more people already on the bed, all getting down to it, things started to blur. If I noticed someone next to me doing something interesting, like the Russian girl holding a cock in each hand, I would get involved. I never met with any refusals: everyone was happy for me to join in when I chose to. It was very easy to move from person to person. I don't know how many guys I had sex with that night, but I wouldn't be exaggerating if I said ten or more. I gave blowjobs to more still.

Not every guy in the room was itching to get involved. Anad was content to watch, and although the Russian's boyfriend eventually stepped in to have sex with her, he showed no interest in me or any of the other girls. Although most couples can't cope with the thought of watching their partner have sex with someone else, these guys clearly got off on it. It was something I saw again and again at parties.

They were not the only voyeurs. I remember noticing an Indian guy standing in a corner on his own. He had his right hand down his trousers and a filthy expression on his face. I wasn't exactly in a position to criticise, but there was something oddly dirty about the image he presented.

After nearly an hour, I decided to take a breather. I took a towel from the bedroom's en suite and went outside to grab a drink. Still red-faced and panting, I sat on the corner of a sofa and marvelled at the apartment. It was massive, with a giant open-plan kitchen/living room. It was a seriously stylish pad, with white walls and furniture, and dark hardwood floors. I felt a bit guilty about the poor owner. He rents out his beautiful apartment for the night in good faith, and what happens? Eighty swingers fuck each other all over the place.

The action had spread to the living room while I was busying myself in the bedroom. I noticed Thomas, the organiser, was playing a prominent, if disturbing, role. He was tall and over forty, with receding hair and a skinny frame. He had dark, predatory eyes and was what could only be described as a creepy, ugly motherfucker. I sat and watched while he tried to coax a slightly overweight girl in her late twenties, who had crashed on another sofa, out of her clothes. She looked barely sober enough to consent and appeared to be only partly taking in what he was saying. His strategy seemed to revolve around using the fact that this was his party as a means of pressurising the girl to have sex with him. His thinking seemed to be that he had let her in for free, so she was pretty much obliged to let him fuck her. I'm not sure if it was his persuasive line of argument or the fact that she was hammered that clinched it for him, but when he started unceremoniously yanking off her jeans she didn't stop him. He was on her like a rat up a drainpipe. She was barely moving or making a sound, just staring with hooded eyes into space. For his part, Thomas didn't seem to give a shite that he was essentially poking a corpse.

Everyone else had been enjoying themselves in an adult, consensual manner but this scumbag had gone too far. He made me feel ill. If he even spoke to me I decided, he would be meeting the hard end of the glass I was drinking from. I went back to the bedroom, and although the better atmosphere in there perked me up a bit, I'd had enough for one night. I grabbed my clothes and told Anad I wanted to leave.

Anad and I were treated like royalty when we were checking into the Four Seasons and Anad treated me even better when we were alone, but my abiding memory of that night is that creep Thomas and his borderline date-rape antics.

Chapter Twelve

I was becoming more and more involved in the scene as the months went by. It was my social life, my hobby, my sex life, my circle of friends. It just took over. It was addictive. People do all kinds of fucked-up things in the search for an adrenalin rush. They jump out of planes, abseil off cliffs or beat each other up in boxing rings; the swinging scene gave me my adrenaline rush.

Swinging was also giving me confidence and that kicked over into other aspects of my life. People were noticing. I was getting far more attention than I used to whenever I went on a normal night out to a bar or club around the city. I was in my old haunt Fibber's one night when a guy I had secretly drooled over at school made a pass at me. I had grown up a bit and I probably looked different than I had the last time he saw me, but not that different. It wasn't the minor physical changes that had occured between my teens and the start of my twenties that had drawn that guy, and the others like him. It was my confidence – confidence swinging had given me. It was driving me out into the world and making me grow as a person. Confidence, I was discovering, can get you very far.

This growth in my confidence made swinging an even more important part of my life, and I was realising that leaving it behind might be difficult. Even when I was deep in the scene it was never something I wanted to do indefinitely. I wanted to get it, whatever 'it' might be, out my system while I was young. I didn't like the idea of turning up to swingers' parties wrinkled and worn, in the hope of getting someone to jump my bones. Plus, buried at the back of my mind, was a desire to one day meet someone, have a normal relationship and live happily ever after.

I got an indication of just how difficult leaving the scene would be when Angelina and I decided to have a sex-free get-together at her place. We had been partying hard and we both felt like we needed a break.

We invited a couple of regular swingers around, on the understanding that nothing beyond a few drinks and a chat would be happening. In the end ten people showed up and our no-sex evening turned into a fuck fest that raged through every room in the house and until the early hours of the morning.

I wasn't the only one hooked. Angelina was far more into it than she probably should have been. Her friend Vicki was another regular. Beyond us three was a core group that could be relied upon to turn up to most events. However, the vast bulk of people who came along would dip their toes into swinging for a few weeks or months before moving on without a backwards glance. It looked to me like those who stayed longer than an initial few months found it hard to leave.

The upside was that I made some good friends from among the regulars, while also meeting a revolving cast of weird and wonderful people who passed through. The more I met, though, the more I worried I would bump into someone I knew. I wasn't ashamed of what I did, but I felt I could do without a relative or a friend of my dad ambling up to me with his cock out at a party before they realised who I was. I once spotted a guy at a meet-and-greet event in a Dublin nightclub who I recognised immediately. He lived around the corner from where I grew up and had gone to my school. He stuck out in my mind because he had always been a bit of an oddball, and that night cemented my view of him. It wasn't the fact that he had gone to a swingers' event that made me think he was strange – it was that he had turned up dressed as a leprechaun.

The oddness of his bright green outfit was heightened by a pair of those weird, toed running shoes, a closely shaved head and bushy beard. He seemed to be the topic of most conversations in the room and I prayed he wouldn't recognise me. Unfortunately, leprechauns apparently have good memories and he twigged who I was within minutes. I was chatting with Angelina and a group of other swingers when he walked straight up to me. 'Do you live on my road?' he asked with a grin.

The leprechaun turned out to be a really funny guy. He didn't give a flying shite about what he looked like or what people thought of him, and it was hard not to admire the chap for it. My respect didn't extend far enough for me to want to sleep with him, however, and he went home alone that night. I remember watching him strutting from the nightclub, with his shiny head and toed runners, still not giving a flying fuck. I think that was his one-and-only taste of the swinging scene. I never saw him again.

Meeting different guys and fucking them eventually got repetitive. The complete emotional detachment, which strips away everything other than the superficial, paper-thin physical side of sex, meant it was bound to happen eventually. It wasn't that I stopped enjoying the sex; it was just that the excitement it had once given me was ebbing away. I had been going to swingers' parties for nearly a year and a half and even they were starting to lose some of their sheen. Sexual satisfaction was easy to come by, but it didn't provide fulfilment. There was a void that this type of sex couldn't fill.

I probably should have walked away at that point, but instead I started pushing myself to take part in more, better and wilder sexual experiences. I kept swinging, and when I did I pushed myself further. I had sex with more people, I went to more parties and I fucked for longer. But there was also something else I wanted to explore. I wanted to go to another fetish night, but not the type where everybody dresses up, has a few drinks and goes home. I hoped that by exploring my kinkier side I might find what I was looking for. I decided to mention it to Angelina. 'I'll go,' she said cheerfully, like I was asking her to come with me to a pet shop to choose a puppy.

We took to the internet and found out about a fetish night organised by two guys who worked in a music shop in Dublin. Angelina dropped by the shop and bought a pair of tickets. It was as simple as that. Even as we put together our plans, I had no idea how the party would go. I certainly had no clue that I would wind up strapped to a table while two doms went to work on me.

When the big night came, I swung by Angelina's to get ready and have a few warm-up drinks. We decided to dress as scandolusly as we could get away with without being arrested on the street. I chose a criminally short, skin-tight leather skirt teamed with a pair of black stockings, the tops of which just peeked out from under my skirt when I sat down. I rounded off the look with knee-high leather boots, a tight, low-cut red vest top lined with black lace and heavy, dark eye make-up.

Angelina wore an equally-short black skirt, and a purple and black corset that gripped her petite frame. She too went for dark make-up, which looked stunning with her exotic Middle Eastern features. My dog collar, the leash of which Angelina was casually swinging while we sipped our drinks and put the finishing touches to our make-up, completed the picture.

Things were not yet underway when we turned up at the slightly spooky old Victorian building where the event was being held. We were welcomed at the door by one of the organisers; he looked to be closing in on the forty mark, and his dark hair was slightly greyed at the temples. But he was handsome, with dark, almost Mediterranean eyes and a strong, lightly stubbled jaw-line. His Clooney-esque look wasn't something I had expected to run into, but I wasn't complaining.

He ushered us inside and took our tickets with a tired smile before closing the door behind us. The doorway opened into a large square room that, apart from an ornate cast-iron fireplace, had been converted into a very modern living room. There were fewer than a dozen people in the room and they were drinking and chatting casually. They took very little notice of us. It could have been the early stages of a birthday party or an office Christmas do, except for the fact that the party-goers were dressed in a weird and wonderful array of fetish outfits.

It was a scary-looking crowd but just like the first fetish party I'd been too, the atmosphere was not at all menacing. We grabbed a drink each from a table in the corner of the room, quickly polished them off and then took a second. Angelina nudged me and nodded towards a door at the opposite side of the room to the one we had come in. A couple, dressed in matching black rubber trousers and black mesh string vests, pulled the door open and disappeared down a flight of stairs.

'That's where the party is on,' said Angelina.

We slammed our drinks, grabbed a third and walked towards the door. I felt a sudden shudder of nervousness. I thought we were already at the party, but the converted stable/gimp-dungeon we found at the bottom of the steps left me reeling.

There were about twenty people downstairs, and most were wearing even more scandalous outfits than the people upstairs. The most shocking among them were the gimps. There was at least a half-dozen of them. I had never seen one of these fabled creatures in person before and I had half wondered if, like unicorns or gremlins, they actually existed outside of works of fiction.

We were approached by the incongruent George Clooney lookalike who welcomed us when we arrived. He had ditched the conservative outfit he wore while on door duty and had changed into a pair of black rubber shorts and a rubber sleeveless v-neck. His change of outfit seemed to have precipitated a similarly seismic shift in his mood. He was suddenly full of life and incapable of removing a white-toothed smile from his face.

He asked us if it was our first time at the event. When we told him it was, he asked about what we were interested in trying. I explained that I was hoping to explore my submissive side.

'Do you have a safe word?' he asked, unnerving perma-grin still on his face.

I had never thought about it, and I still wasn't sure if I needed one. The event, the people at it and the terrifying array of torture-chamber-style paraphernalia was scaring the shit out of me. Just in case, I decided to pick a word. It needed to be something with no sexual connotations whatsoever. But this isn't as easy as you might imagine. 'Rainbow,' I said after a pause.

George seemed to like it and both he and Angelina erupted into laughter. It was a strange choice but I thought it was a good one. There can be very few sexual scenarios in which the subject of rainbows would crop up, so I felt happy that it couldn't possibly be mistaken for anything other than me calling a halt.

I know most people would reel at the sight of this type of stuff, but I wanted to try it. It was new, fresh, exciting and scary enough to get my adrenaline pumping. It appealed to me in the same way as meeting guys from the net once had, and the way swinging did when I first got started. But the sheer weirdness of the scene in that room was threatening to cripple me with anxiety. Angelina clicked her leash onto the collar around my neck and the action got underway.

People went on doing their things in various corners of the building right through until 3 or 4 a.m., but Angelina and I went back upstairs around midnight. We were lying on a bed, thinking about heading home, when a couple I had noticed earlier flopped down next to us. They were an interesting pair. Philip was tall, another skinhead, and he had an odd handlebar moustache. Ciara was dressed in a black and red corset that came to just under her bust, leaving her chest fully exposed. She had a pretty face, deathly white skin and dark, extravagant eye make-up. Her look was made even more extreme by a black, oriental style shoulder-length wig with a geometric fringe. She told us she was an ex-stripper and loved cooking. Philip was a few years older than her, but they seemed to be crazy about each other.

As strange as they appeared, they spoke mostly about their jobs, their home and about having to go home to their kids the next day. They told us they were really enjoying having some time to themselves for a change. During daylight hours they were just like everyone else.

It was a fucked-up night, but certainly not one I regretted. It was something different and I had fun trying it out. I got to explore another side of myself and to find out more about what I did and didn't like. But although it was a positive experience, it made me realise that I was no die-hard sadomasochist. I loved it and wanted more, but there would be no getting me into a gimp suit.

I exchanged numbers with Philip and Ciara and we texted regularly over the days and weeks that followed. They both preferred to be dominant in the bedroom, which I'm sure presented problems. Maybe this was why they liked to introduce third parties, so they could share a submissive. I told them I was sold on the idea, so we planned a mini S&M session at their place.

They had a house hidden away in the fields and pastures of County Louth and although I liked and trusted them, I decided I would bring Angelina along just in case. She was happy to oblige and we arranged to meet Ciara in the city; Angelina would drive and Ciara would direct us to their home. She turned up to meet us dressed in a second, slightly less revealing corset. She had donned another wig, this one a dark purple colour. I asked her where she got her outfits from, and she told me they came mostly from online shops and that she dressed like that all the time.

It was just as well we had decided to pick her up – their small home was in some obscure corner of the wee county, in the middle of absolutely nowhere. It was a good fifteen minutes' drive from the nearest sign of life. It was no wonder they were driven to kinky sexual practices – there was fuck all else to do out there.

Philip answered the door dressed in a pair of jeans and a T-shirt, and the night kicked off with us getting stuck into the drink we'd brought and they had laid on. Ciara busied herself in the kitchen before calling us in for dinner. She had made pizza and we clinked glasses and complimented her cooking like we were on an episode of *Come Dine With Me*.

This pair was full of surprises. Ciara explained how she had been a lesbian as long as she could remember and that she had only ever had girlfriends before she met Philip. He was her first boyfriend. The girl was a bit nuts but she was really nice. They were a fun couple.

We had been drinking steadily for two hours when Philip suggested we take a look at what he had done with their upstairs bedroom. It sounded like the worst chat-up line in history, but the bedroom was cool. He had a huge sound system with speakers in the four corners of the room and, after flicking a switch on a massive hi-fi system, they blared deep house music at ear-splitting volume. Thick black curtains prevented much light from getting into the room, but I could make out enough to see he had put together a mini version of the 'dungeon' that served as the venue for the party we met at. He had a similar array of sex toys arranged on shelves and dangling from hooks on the blood-red walls. All that remained was for us to make use of the place.

Among Philip's bag of tricks was a length of rope specifically made for tying people up; it was soft to the touch and didn't irritate or mark the skin. He pulled it from a hook on the wall and told me to lie on the bed. I did as I was told as we slipped into our dom and sub roles. While he unravelled the rope, Ciara started yanking off my clothes. I expected to be tied to the bed, but instead Philip set about binding my ankles and arms behind my back with the one piece of rope. It seemed complicated, but he knew what he was doing and I was soon completely vulnerable to whatever these people felt like doing to me. I couldn't move, but the ropes weren't painfully tight. Ciara went to the wall and took down a leather whip similar to the one that had been used on me in the dungeon. I was lying face down, and she started gently running the strands of the whip up and down my back. Then, without notice, she thwacked me on the ass with it. I felt a hot sting that settled into a now familiar pleasurable warmth.

Angelina sat watching while Ciara handed the whip over to Philip. He caught me by surprise: the first thing he did was lean in and ask if I was okay. When I said I was fine, he started lashing me with the whip even harder than Ciara had. While I was still being whipped, Angelina took me by the hair and tilted my head back. Philip had paused to take his cock out, and he moved around the bed towards me. Angelina slapped me gently on the face, which I took as my queue to open my mouth. I was hog-tied on a bed so I wasn't in a position to refuse. I opened up while Angelina pushed my head up and down on Philip's dick.

Angelina and Ciara started playing around with each other while Philip got onto the bed behind me. After whipping me hard across the ass one more time, I felt him lie down on top of me and ease his cock inside. He took hold of a handful of my hair, and started to fuck me hard and fast. I loved being so helpless; it was completely intoxicating. Before he finished, I noticed Ciara retrieving something from the wall.

'You're going to love this,' Ciara said in a somewhat sinister tone. I felt Philip pull out and climb off me and then I felt something else, far bigger than his cock, being pushed roughly inside me. It was painful, but I could just about take it. At first I thought Ciara was using a big dildo on me, but the way the bed shifted made me realise what she was doing – she was about to fuck me with some sort of gargantuan strap-on. Her lesbian tendencies were evidently making a return, and she delighted in fucking me as hard as she could. I started to tingle all over and I was soon cumming in long, trembling surges. 'That's enough,' said Philip, pulling Ciara away from me.

I noticed that while Ciara liked to be dominant with other people, she was very much the submissive in her relationship with Philip. Angelina eased me onto my back, and started sucking on my nipples and playing with my pussy with her fingers. In doing so, she gave me a view of what the other two were getting up to. They were going crazy. Philip had pinned his girlfriend face down on the bed. He was gripping her neck with one hand and using the other to guide his cock straight into her asshole. He wasn't exactly being gentle, and her face was contorting in spasms of pain and pleasure. After a few strokes, he started hammering her mercilessly. It was quite shocking to see, but they were a couple so I guessed that they knew each other's limits. Still, I was surprised. I found it strange that a girl who had spent most of her life living as a lesbian would be so into getting fucked in the ass.

Ciara announced that she had something to show us. Then, she bounded downstairs and into the back garden – still completely naked. The rest of us pulled on some clothes and walked after her. What in the name of God was this woman going to do next?

We stepped out into the garden to see Ciara crouched down on the ground. She looked like she was trying to set fire to something. Angelina and I looked at each other, wondering if it might be time to sprint from the premises. When Ciara stood up she had a slim chain in each hand, both of which had a flaming ball at the end. I had seen these things before; they were called *poi*. Ciara was a fire juggler.

She swung the chains around, creating elegant

arcs and patterns in the blackness of the Louth countryside while Angelina filmed it on her mobile phone. There was something otherworldly about seeing this ghostly-pale woman swinging balls of fire around her. At 3 a.m. Completely bare-arse naked. In Louth.

Chapter Thirteen

I was cruising around the swinger's website one evening when I spotted a familiar, bearded face. It had been years since I'd seen the guy but there was no doubt in my mind – it really was him. It was Luke – my first major crush and the person I had lost my virginity to. I hadn't thought about him in years. The fucker had broken my heart so putting him out of my mind had been no mean feat. But rather than bringing back thoughts of the angsty, teenage tears I'd pushed into my pillow because of what he had done to me, I found myself smiling and remembering those electrifying afternoons in my old bedroom. He hadn't just been the first person I'd had sex with. He was also the first person I'd had rough sex with. On reflection, I probably owed the submissiveness I later developed, at least in part, to this guy.

It took me a while to even consider the strangeness

of the fact that he was on a swingers' website. I would never have imaged that he'd be the type. Signing up for a site like this smacks of effort. The Luke I knew was too cool, and too lazy, for anything like that, surely. I squinted at the image on the screen – his head was turned slightly to the side and his long, dark hair partly covered his face, but there was no doubt. It was Luke all right. People change, I guess.

I sat there for a while agonising over whether I should contact him. If I had come across him on Facebook I wouldn't have hesitated, but a re-introduction via a swingers' website seemed a bigger deal. It would cut out the need for a 'How are you?' from either of us, anyway. The answer was already obvious. Horny.

I knew it was probably a bad idea. He had deliberately set me up so I would see him with some prissy wannabe cheerleader when he knew I was absolutely infatuated with him. Luke had humiliated me. But as much as I tried to focus on the hurt I felt all those years ago, my mind kept drifting back to that first orgasm I had with him. I didn't have the experience to recognise it for what it was back then, but Luke had been a kinky fucker. He had a definite fondness for slapping, hair-pulling, tossing me around the bedroom like a ragdoll and generally fucking me like I owed him money. Was he still like that? Was he worse? Where had his sexual journey taken him? I held my breath, typed a quick 'hello stranger' and sat back into my chair. I guess I would be finding out.

I dived onto the computer the next day to see if Luke had responded. For all I knew he wouldn't recognise me. Worse, he had rejected me once – maybe he still wouldn't be interested. By the grace of God, buried in a stack of emails from various randomers, was a message from him.

'Wow, Katie – fancy meeting you here.'

So, Luke and I started chatting online again. It was like we had just started from scratch. Apart from occasionally erupting into mock outrage and calling him an arsehole for being such a complete dick to me when we were younger, it was like it had never happened. I was just playing around when I gave him a hard time about it and getting over it just felt like the grown-up thing to do. Sure, it hurt at the time but we were both a lot younger. I didn't really give a shit about it any more so I didn't see any reason why I should pretend I did. And, I wasn't looking for a relationship from the guy now. As fun as it was to feel those familiar tingles from my teens again, it wasn't going to go anywhere – if anything did happen, it would be just for fun.

As we chatted, I was amazed by how clearly it brought back memories of the time I'd spent camped out in front of my computer in my mother's spare room while Luke tapped out effortless nonchalance in some dreary all-night internet café. He had an apartment these days. And a job – he worked in IT. His life turned around when he had moved to Manchester and, with some help from the presumably guilt-ridden parents who had left the kid homeless, enrolled in college there. He graduated and had only recently returned home.

So what in the name of God was he doing on a swingers' site?

'That's a silly question, Katie, no?' said Luke.

He was right. He was there for the same thing I was. There was only one thing for it – we would have to meet.

Now that we were both grown-ups, when and where we met was no longer dictated by my ma's work schedule. Still, I didn't want to just run around to his place to jump his bones. I had really enjoyed chatting with him again and I felt like a drink somewhere might be a good idea.

'Let's go to Fibber's,' I said.

I was running the risk of going into nostalgia overload, but Luke was the reason why I had got so obsessed with that bar, and that scene, in the first place. But then my age meant that I'd never actually had the opportunity to go for a drink with the chap there.

'Sure,' said Luke. 'I haven't been there in years.'

We arranged to meet the following Friday night and although we kept chatting online pretty much every evening, the wait was killing me. When the night finally came, I spent hours fussing over my clothes and make-up. I looked a lot different than I did when we first met. I was an awkward teen still carrying a lot of puppy fat. That was now long gone, and I the rollercoaster of a time I'd had meant I was no longer a shrinking violet. Last time out I was a shy, chubby teen. Now I was a confident, grown woman.

Luke hadn't yet arrived when I turned up, so I grabbed a drink and drummed my fingers anxiously on the bar. I knew I was being ridiculous but I couldn't help being nervous. Seeing an ex-boyfriend is a minefield; more so when you really want to fuck the guy again. But what if he didn't find me attractive? Worse, what if he stood me up? But I was excited, too. And I was curious about how he would look. He was heading into his late twenties now and I wanted to see in person how the years had been treating him. Thankfully, I didn't have to wait long. I was barely halfway through my first drink when he ambled slowly inside.

His hair was slightly shorter than it had been, his beard was trimmed a bit neater, and his clothes, while still very much rocker, were less ragged than the stuff he used to wear. Understandably so – he wasn't a hobo these days. Beyond that, the guy looked remarkably similar to how he had the last time I saw him. If anything, he had filled out. He was still quite lean, but he had lost any trace of the awkwardness he had carried himself with when he was younger.

'I can't believe how well you look,' he said after ordering a drink and plonking down next to me.

'I'll take that as a compliment,' I said with a smile, as Luke blushed slightly and stumbled over his words in an attempt to reassure me that this was how he had meant it.

It was funny. I'd never been able to make him squirm like that when we were younger. Or if I had, I certainly never noticed.

I could say we spent that evening chatting away like we had never been apart, but that wasn't quite the case. Sure, the old attraction was there on my part but he seemed far more interested than he had first time out. Maybe he had just grown to be a little less aloof than he once was, or maybe it was because he was dealing with a very different Katie. As a teenager, I was in awe of this guy to the point of being intimidated and I had to fight to get my words out. Now, I was more comfortable in myself. I had handled bigger and badder boys than him by the roomful and he held no fear for me now. Luke quickly picked up on that – and I think he was attracted by it.

When kicking out time came, I was in no mood to play games.

'My place or yours?' I said when we stood to leave, slipping two of my fingers behind his belt and pulling him towards me.

'Let's go for mine.'

I wanted to dive on him as soon as we were in the back of a taxi but Luke had other ideas.

'Wait,' he said sternly, swiping my hand away from his crotch and staring intently at me. 'Wait until I say so.'

I had to fight down a grin that wanted to burst across my face. I was right about Luke – he was still a kinky bastard.

'Sorry, sir,' I said, putting my hands on my lap and looking at the floor.

'I share this place with a flatmate,' said Luke, shoving open the door to his apartment. 'But we're the only ones home tonight.'

We were fighting our way out of our clothes and stumbling towards the sofa before the before the door had swung closed behind us. I had forgotten how big this guy was compared to me; I felt tiny in his arms as we kissed.

Then, out of nowhere, Luke broke away and took a step away from me. I felt suddenly exposed as I stood there in the dimly-lit room as he folded his arms and looked me up and down. I reflexively grabbed my top from the ground and held it to my chest.

'Drop it,' said Luke firmly. I put my hands by my sides and let it drop to the floor.

'Turn around,' he snapped. I did as I was told.

Luke walked towards me from behind. I could feel his breath on the back of my neck and he stood close to me. Suddenly, he pushed me hard. I flew forward and broke my fall by putting my two hands out onto the sofa. Before I had a time to react Luke clamped a giant hand onto my waist and worked his cock inside me with the other. I inhaled sharply as he forced himself roughly into me.

Luke wasn't in the mood for foreplay, or for gentle love-making. He slammed me hard, pulling me onto him by my hips to increase the force. I wanted to show him how tough, experienced and in control I could be, but my legs were already starting to tremble. An involuntary moan escaped my lips as he grabbed a handful of hair and continued to pound. I screwed my eyes shut and dug my nails into the sofa as a hot, deep orgasm started to crackle and spread from the pit of my stomach to the tips of my fingers and toes.

Luke quickened his pace. He was breathing heavily. He was going to cum too. The room swam, my toes curled and a rush of ecstasy blasted through me. I felt Luke pull out and the heat of his cum spraying onto the small of my back. I gazed at Luke as the room came back to focus. It was every bit as good as I remembered.

Afterwards, when the two of us had made our way to his bed, I decided I just had to ask.

'So … why were you such a dick when we went out? You knew I was crazy about you back then, right?'

'I had an idea,' said Luke.

I let the silence hang. I wanted an answer, and I was determined to get one. Luke shifted uncomfortably. 'Well, you were a different kettle of fish back then, Katie. For a start, you didn't actually speak. I was starting to wonder if you were a mute.'

That was true, in fairness. I could barely get the words out when speaking to my own mother back then.

'You came across as pretty mature when we chatted online but you were different in person. I kept waiting for you to come out of your shell, but it just didn't happen.'

Luke explained that my shyness had made him start to feel guilty about seeing someone so much younger than him. It sounded a little bit like he was covering his arse, but I decided I could let him get away with it. It all seemed so remote. I had got over it in a few weeks and now, I felt I could laugh about it.

'But you did have one thing going for you,' Luke continued.

'What was that?'

'You made a serious fucking sandwich.'

Luke and I started to see quite a bit of each other. We cut out the Fibber's foreplay and went back to either his or mine every other weekend. But although we clicked in the bedroom and got on like a house on fire outside it, I wasn't interested into getting into anything serious. For a start, I was still seeing other guys and although I never asked him outright, I got the impression I wasn't the only girl in his life. I was also concerned that shackling what we had with the status of the 'relationship' tag might spoil the fun we were having. And we were having a lot of fun.

Over the weeks that followed, we began to sink further into our respective bedroom personas. He became more domineering while I became more submissive.

I'm sure there are feminists out there who will spontaneously combust with fury if they ever read this, but there was something else I wanted to try. Even by my standards, it was way, way out there. I wanted to explore role play – and one scenario in particular appealed to me. I wanted Luke to go beyond normal domination. I wanted him to take complete control. I wanted him to force the issue.

There's a name for this type of thing – 'rape play'. In reality, the concept is a complete oxymoron. There's no playing involved in an actual rape, and there's no actual rape involved if you're just playing. But I wanted to act out a scenario where Luke attempted to have sex with me and I would resist. Then, ultimately, he would overpower me and get his way. The idea of actually being raped by some stranger is just as abhorrent and horrifying to me as it is to any other woman. I didn't harbour any fantasies about being jumped by some predatory scumbag. As far as I was concerned this was just a harmless and completely consensual game I wanted to play with a guy I was seeing. Sure, he was going to be forcing me – but only because I was giving him permission to.

'I could do that,' said Luke when I finally worked up the nerve to broach the topic. 'But how does it work?'

I explained that I thought it we could do it at my place when there was nobody else home. He could knock at the door, I could answer it and he could burst inside. So that's what we did.

I picked a night when my apartment would be very much empty. The last thing I needed was a horrified housemate bursting in and plunging a breadknife into Luke's back. We had run over what we were going to do and how we were going to do it so when the night came, Luke was at home waiting on a text from me to give him the green light.

I punched 'Ready when you are' into my phone and hit 'send'.

I was tingling all over with anticipation. Every time I thought of what was about to happen – my fantasy of being completely one hundred percent taken over – I felt giddy and couldn't wipe the smile off my face. But I was a little nervous, too. I mean, this was a pretty crazy way to spend an evening. I reassured myself by remembering that it was, after all, just a game. We had agreed a safe word so if it got too much, he went too far or if I just got scared, I could call a halt. I trusted Luke.

Then doorbell rang. I took a deep breath and attempted to slip into character. Who could be calling at this late hour?

I pulled the door open slightly and peered through the gap. My jaw almost hit the floor. Luke was clean-shaven, he had slicked his hair back and he was wearing a black suit. He looked, as I imagine was his intention, like a completely different person. My surprise at seeing him like that knocked my concentration and I had to remind myself that I didn't know him.

'Can I help you?' I said, fighting down my desire for him in a bid to feign concern.

Luke stepped back and looked left and right to see if anyone was paying attention. Then he burst through the door and shoved it closed behind him.

'What the fuck are you doing?' I said, wondering if he was going to be able to keep this thing on track.

Luke grinned slightly as he walked towards me. He was enjoying himself too. 'You should be careful who you answer the door to at this hour,' he said calmly.

I turned to run upstairs but he caught me by the hair and pinned me against the wall by the throat. I was wearing a white office shirt and he ripped it open with one hand before throwing me onto the stairs.

'No!' I screamed, doing my best to play my part. My mind was swimming. I wanted to scream at him to fuck me.

Luke moved in, unbuckling his trousers. I spun around and attempted to get away by crawling up the stairs but he caught me by an ankle and dragged me roughly back down.

'Please,' I said, which was a little closer to the truth. Luke said nothing but kept his eyes fixed on mine. They had an icy coolness to him that I hadn't seen before and for a moment I was lost in the game. For a second, it really felt like he was in control. He was going to do whatever he wanted with me and I didn't have a say.

He pulled my trousers off me in a single movement and manoeuvred himself on top of me. I fought as hard as I could to keep him off, or at least from penetrating me. I kicked my legs, slapped him across the face, pulled his hair and dug my nails into his arms and chest. I fought as long as I could, but he was too heavy and too strong. When Luke felt the fight going out of me, he pinned me by the throat with one hand and guided himself inside me with the other.

'Don't!' I said breathlessly, staring back at him.

I lay there exhausted while he fucked me, my resistance reduced to spitting insults. Luke fucked me hard and rough and I soon felt that familiar warm, prickling sensation undulate through me. I wanted to scream the house down but I didn't want to give 'my attacker' the satisfaction of hearing me cum. So I screwed my eyes shut, bit down on my bottom lip and let the waves of pleasure rip up and down my spine without making a sound. Luke was as turned on as I was by the scenario we had concocted and he came in a shuddering burst moments later.

I realised afterwards that we hadn't talked about what we would do once he had finished. I lay there panting, wondering what Luke would do next. His eyes still had that alien coldness to them and he stared harshly at me. Then he pulled himself out of me and stood up. Lying at his feet, the guy looked taller than ever. From this angle, he was like a certified giant. Then, he buckled himself up and walked calmly to the door without saying a word.

'You bastard!' I shouted, struggling to suppress an involuntary giggle that came bubbling up.

Lying on my bed after Luke left, I thought about how lucky I had been. I had come up with an absolutely outrageous sexual fantasy but rather than suppressing and ignoring it, I was in a position to not only broach the subject with the guy I was sleeping with, but to actually make it happen. Sure, my fantasy had been desperately politically incorrect but it wasn't going to harm anyone and we both had a good time doing it.

I thought about the people walking around on the other side of my bedroom window and about what fantasies they might be harbouring. I'm sure some had a partner they trusted enough to share them with but many wouldn't. They would never get to talk about the things they wanted to do never mind experience them. And for what? Shame or embarrassment or worry. They would take them to the grave. They would no doubt pity me for the lifestyle I was leading but I felt a little bit sad for them.

Luke texted me later that night to ask if I was okay. He told me he had really enjoyed our little experiment and suggested we meet again the following night. I was delighted too. Luke had been brilliant. He deserved a fucking Oscar for that performance.

The following night, lying in Luke's bed after doing our best to tire each other out, I decided to try to find out more of his story. I knew how he had got himself back on track, got an education and found a good job, but there was another big question mark about another aspect of his life which was a lot more relevant to our 'relationship'. He had seemingly gone from being the comparatively normal guy with a slight preference for rough sex I had first met to a full-blown BDSM enthusiast.

As it turned out, his 'development' had come about largely due to a girl he met in while in the UK. She was petite, cute, in her early twenties and from a well-off family. Luke met her in college and beyond coming across as a little bit shy at first, she had seemed just like any other girl her age. Until their friendship became physical.

Luke told me that right from the first time they slept together, she encouraged him to be rough with her. She begged him to pull her hair, slap her and toss her around like a rag doll. For his part, Luke loved it. He was being given free rein to explore his domineering tendencies by a beautiful young girl who loved every second of it. They had discovered they had something very unusual in common that neither of them could get enough of. I couldn't help but raise an eyebrow as Luke told me the story. It sounded remarkably similar to how the guy was when we first started sleeping together.

'Will you let me explain?' said Luke, picking up on my sceptical reaction.

He went on to tell me about how things began to spiral as the weeks and months went on. She began demanding that Luke go further. She wanted to be bitten. She wanted to be spat on. She wanted to be punched in the face. Whenever he cranked things up a gear, her demands would simply become more severe. There was no end to it and Luke was worried about where it would end. His girl, on the other hand, was changing. She reacted furiously whenever he hesitated and he started to wind up on the receiving end of the violence. She was abusive when he wasn't abusive enough. What he had taken for submissiveness initially was beginning to look like something very different.

Luke enjoyed rough sex and being dominant, but there was a line. He felt that punching a girl in the face crossed it. He wasn't willing to do anything that was going to injure any girl – let alone one he cared about. For a start, he could have seriously hurt her. He explained that she was tiny and he worried he would break her. She was already covered in bruises and Luke hadn't gone half as far as she had begged him to.

Luke had another concern, too. She was unstable. What if he did what she asked and she came away with a black eye? It would put him in a very vulnerable position. People would ask questions and she could very easily use it against him if the mood took her. Luke didn't trust her enough to get so deep into it.

Eventually, Luke called a halt. What had started as a fun secret the pair shared had turned into a horribly abusive and patently unhealthy relationship. She had cried and wailed and threatened and eventually, Luke decided it would be best if he returned to Ireland.

But while he was forced to end the relationship for both their sakes, it had left an impression on him. Before it had gone too far, before his girl's submissiveness had morphed into a fucked-up type of dominance, he had treasured their time together. The sex had been beyond anything he had experienced before and he wanted to replicate it. He had discovered a world he wanted more of.

'Wow,' I said when Luke had finished. I was surprised Luke had opened up in the way he did. I was even more surprised that he had been willing to go ahead with my pretend rape scenario after his bad experiences with his ex. It felt like he trusted me.

Luke and I had got on so well since we met up second time around that it seemed like a steady, traditional boyfriend/girlfriend relationship beckoned. But while we were both very fond of each other and we had a great time between the sheets, things were never going to go in that direction. For a start, even when we were seeing each other regularly, we were both still seeing other people. I was still going to parties. The foundations were just too fucked up to build anything substantial. Inevitably, after a few months, we began to see less of each other.

Chapter Fourteen

*G*reg was born and bred Irish, but with a distinctly Mediterranean look. He used to DJ at some of the bigger swingers' parties. He would occasionally take a break from spinning tracks to dive into the action and on one such occasion, we hooked up. We went back to my place that night and although we exchanged numbers the next day, I wasn't expecting to hear from him again. About a month later, at 3 a.m., I woke up to the sound of someone banging the shit out of my front door. At first I didn't register what the noise was; and then my phone rang. 'I'm outside your house.' I recognised Greg's voice straight away. 'Let me in.'

I didn't want him waking up my housemates so I told him I would be right down. I brought him in and he flopped onto the sofa, completely wasted. I asked him what he was doing turning up at 3 a.m., and he told me he had got himself into trouble. He explained how he had got into an argument at a club and punched some guy in the face. He ran off when the guards showed up. He looked rattled by what had happened.

I waited for Greg to offer some sort of explanation as to why he had turned up at my door, but none was forthcoming. He eventually asked if he could stay. I was worried how he might react if I refused, so I told him he could, adding that nothing would be happening. He crashed out and was snoring within minutes. He woke up early the next morning and headed on his way without much by way of chat. When I was on my way out the door later that day, my neighbour, a friendly little woman in her eighties, called me over. She told me that the night before, she had heard a guy outside our house shouting about how he was going to smash our windows if he wasn't allowed in.

She told me she was out of bed with the phone in her hand ready to call the guards, when I opened the door. Greg had seemed normal, but turned out to be a violent asshole who had punched someone in the face and then threatened to smash his way into my house. It was scary, and it was enough to make me have second thoughts about what I had been doing.

I spent the next day thinking about where I had been headed. I was deep, deep into a very extreme lifestyle, and of late it wasn't making me as happy as it once did. It wasn't just the unwelcome addition of freaks like Greg that bothered me. I had somehow got to a point where being strapped to a leather table and whipped while people in gimp suits wandered around the room on all fours was a normal night out. But where did it end? What if that got old? What was next? I was running out of boundaries to push.

I had gone into the scene with my eyes open. I wanted to experience everything it had to offer but I also wanted to get it out of my system while I was young, before moving on. I felt like I was quickly arriving at that stage. The underground sex scene was fun, but it was full-on and it was tiring. Even when I was blissed out at the wildest of parties, I knew what I was doing wasn't normal. I could justify it to myself and to others in all sorts of ways, but deep down I knew I had to stop at some point.

That meaningless, emotionless aspect of the sex I had been having was looming ever larger in my mind. I had to seriously question whether I had desensitised myself to the emotional side of sex to a point where I would never be able to have a normal relationship. In fact, the idea of being in one had not only lost the repulsiveness it once had, but it was actually starting to appeal. I liked the idea of being with someone I really cared about and who cared about me too.

I was also worried about the amount of drink I had been putting away on a regular basis. Drink and swinging went hand in hand for me and I knew there would be no way I could go to parties sober. If drink was to go, swinging would have to go with it.

It would be hard to leave. I had met so many cool people and made some good friends. I didn't feel I would have to detach myself from everyone I had met through swinging but I knew I would be moving in a different direction, and it was unlikely I would remain in touch with many of them.

I made my mind up; I'd had enough. After nearly two years of what was probably the wildest sex any twenty-two-year-old Irish girl has ever had, I was going to call time. But I was going to go out with a bang.

Angelina decided she was going to mark my birthday by calling in her A-list swingers and she chose the same hotel she had used for her own party. Because it was close to Halloween, we decided to make it a fancy dress party. After some deliberation, I went for a Lara Croft outfit.

The night didn't get off to a great start. I had recently come across a guy called Marcus on a dating site and although I had only met him in person a handful of times, things had been going well. I was even coming round to the previously unthinkable idea: that it could actually go somewhere. Then, out of nowhere, he announced he had seen my profile on a swingers' website. I wasn't upset that he had discovered my other life; I wasn't exactly secretive about it. But his knowing I was a swinger did make me shove aside any notions of a relationship. When the time came to get couply, I didn't want to do it with someone with any involvement or interest in the scene. But that didn't mean we couldn't still have a good time together.

In the end, I decided to ask Marcus if he wanted to go to a swingers' party with me. If he had been nosing around on a swingers' site, he was obviously interested, so when he agreed I suggested we make my birthday party his first outing on the scene. He decided he wasn't going to drink that night so he swung by in his car to pick me up. The plan was that we would drop by Angelina's place and then the three of us would go to the hotel.

Angelina was in her normal jovial mood when we arrived, but it was becoming clear that there was something bothering my date. We were barely through Angelina's door when Marcus announced that he had left something in his car. He ran back outside – and drove off.

I thought he had decided to drive to a garage, maybe to buy cigarettes or condoms or something, so I didn't think much of it at first. Then my phone bleeped. It was Marcus texting to say he was 'too freaked out' by the whole thing and couldn't go ahead with it. I called to see if he was okay and to explain that tonight was a birthday party first and a swingers' party second. He didn't need to do anything – he could hang around for the birthday part and leave if the sex left him cold. He wasn't having it; there was no way he was coming back. The guy couldn't get off the phone fast enough.

It was a shock. Marcus had been mooching around swingers' sites even before he met me, and he had agreed enthusiastically when I suggested he come to the party. Plus, he was a nice guy and I enjoyed hanging out with him. We had a lot of fun together, both inside and outside the bedroom. I couldn't believe he had just freaked out and driven off. I was quite pissed off with him. The guy was in his mid-twenties. He was an adult and I felt he should have been able for it, but he just chickened out.

All I could do was get on with the party without him. That was the good thing about not getting emotionally attached to guys: even when they did something stupid and let you down, you could brush it off and move on instantly.

After a couple of pre-party drinks in Angelina's, we took a taxi to the hotel and the first arrivals showed up minutes after we'd checked in. I wasn't expecting many to dress up, but quite a few did. One American guy came dressed normally but he whipped off his jacket to reveal a Superman costume underneath. Oddly, another couple turned up dressed as school children.

When the full crowd had arrived, Angelina took out her camera and started shooting pictures. For one shot, the guys lined up and I lay across their arms, like in a burlesque. I hadn't told anyone I planned to make this my last party, not even Angelina. I was a little emotional about closing the door on what had been such a pivotal part of my life. So I poured myself a drink and pulled Superman by the belt into one of the bedrooms while the crowd whooped and cheered.

The party wound down at around 4 a.m. when four or five of the group headed home, leaving a couple of die-hards drinking in the sitting room. The rest of us crashed out together in the bedrooms. It's a strange sight – a group of swingers curling up together and going to sleep at the end of a night – but that's how it was. I suppose that was just the level of familiarity that had developed among the regulars at Angelina's parties. Dozing off to sleep, surrounded by the naked men and women I had shared my body with for nearly two years, I knew it was over. But while I have stuck without regret to my decision, I was to have one last dalliance with Ireland's underground sex scene, and it would land me on every radio station in the country.

Chapter Fifteen

I met Rob at a barbeque a few months after I broke from the scene. We were talking towards the end of the night, at that stage when lips loosen and you mention things that you probably wouldn't otherwise, when we fell on the topic of swinging. I'm not sure how the subject came up, but when it did I let slip that I had some experience of it. Rob's ears pricked up, not surprisingly – he was a journalist.

He explained how he was working for an online magazine for men called Joe.ie, a sort of web-based *FHM* for Irish lads, and that they had been running stories on various aspects of Ireland's underground sex scene. They had already investigated prostitution and run interviews with dominatrices, strippers and porn stars. The articles were hugely successful and readers flooded to the site, so they were hoping to look at swinging next. Rob had been trying to get an invite to a swingers' party for months, but had so far drawn a blank. He had joined a number of swingers' sites, but he ran into the same problem most single guys do: if you don't know the person organising it, you better have a girl to bring with you.

'I can help,' I said, out of sheer mischievousness more than anything else.

By then Angelina had stopped organising her parties but Thomas was still as busy as ever on the scene and I still had his number. The problem was that putting in a good word for Rob wouldn't be enough to get him in. I wasn't exactly Thomas's biggest fan. I hadn't gone to many of his parties, and at the ones I did attend I avoided the guy like the plague. So I suggested that rather than just recommending Rob, I bring him along to a party, so he would have a girl with him.

We spent what remained of the evening chatting excitedly about how we could make it work. Rob was concerned he might stick out like a sore thumb if he didn't get involved, but I reassured him by explaining how there were always plenty of voyeurs, plus a few newbies who couldn't quite bring themselves to get stuck in. Non-participation wouldn't be a problem. We swapped numbers and over the next few days, went about putting our plan into action.

Rob and I planned to pose as a couple. I texted Thomas to say I wanted to come to a party with my new boyfriend. Just to be sure, I told him Rob wasn't interested in doing anything himself but just wanted to watch me being with other guys. Thomas was fine with it, and beyond a reminder that Rob would still have to pay an entry fee for the privilege of 'seeing me in action' even if he wasn't going to get involved, he was happy to extend an invite to his next party. 'Great,' said a smiling Rob when I told him about Thomas's text. 'I'll be the perviest bloke at the swingers' party.'

The event was to take place in another short-term rental apartment, this time in Dublin's south inner city. Rob swung by to collect me in a taxi and, after stopping at an off-licence for a bottle of vodka, we headed towards the address. The building was a typical Celtic-Tiger-era apartment block – swanky and half-empty. Voices were audible from down the hall as soon as we got out of the lift. The apartment door had been left ajar, so Rob pushed it open and we walked straight in. The large, two-bedroom apartment was packed with about thirty-five people sipping drinks and chatting nervously with other party-goers. We were met with that familiar meat-market moment when the crowd turned to make its appraisal of the two latest arrivals.

We headed straight for the relative safety of the kitchen. Despite noticing one or two familiar faces, I felt like I was seeing the scene through fresh eyes. It all felt new and strange, like this was something I had never been a part of. I couldn't believe how nervous being there was making me.

One of the first people we spoke with was Jenny; an expensively put together, late-thities yummy mummy who had arrived with her husband. Her expensive clothes, haughty air and posh accent made it obvious which side of the tracks she was from. With the hellos out of the way she launched straight into a soliloquy about how she had been forced to take a break from swinging because she had just had a baby. Three weeks earlier. Rob just about kept a straight face but he couldn't resist mouthing 'Oh my God!' at me when Jenny turned away.

Rob told me he was half expecting a room filled with sweaty, over-amorous and over-weight menopausal women but he seemed pleasantly surprised. Instead, the female half of the room was made up of a mixed bag of girls, many of whom would have done well in any bar.

There was one glaring exception. There was a tall, rail-thin woman of about thirty milling around the edges of the party like a circling shark. Her face was plastered in sloppily applied make-up and her arms were marked by discoloured, amateurish, Indian ink tattoos. She looked like a heroin addict. While nobody had yet done anything beyond make casual conversation, she appeared to be suffering from a rapidly escalating case of the green-eyed monster.

The girl's aggression was building and I overheard her mutter snide comments about the appearance of some of the other girls who had come along. The situation wasn't helped by the fact that she was already steaming drunk. She started to argue with the guy who had come along with her, appearing to take exception to the fact that he was taking an interest in other girls. I got the impression that he had maybe talked her into coming along to a swingers' party because he needed a girl to go, and she agreed because she liked him. It certainly looked that way because he seemed to have little or no interest in her, while she was looking set to hit the roof whenever he looked sideways. Things went from bad to worse when she stood up too quickly and a combination of her high-heels and a patch of liquid on the tiles sent her crashing to the floor. Now she was uncomfortable, jealous, embarrassed and angry.

This catastrophe was the last straw for her male companion. He quietly helped her to her feet and then walked away, leaving her on her own. Going home probably would have been the sensible thing for her to do, but then she wouldn't be around to keep an eye on her man. So instead she decided to follow him from one part of the house to another while he ducked into bathrooms and hid behind plant pots on the balcony.

Nearly two hours after we arrived there was still no obvious sign of action. The party-goers scattered around the kitchen, sitting room and balcony were all still fully clothed. That said, the crowd was sparser than it had been earlier, which could mean only one thing. I decided to investigate, and I picked my way through the pack towards the bedrooms. The light was on in one of the rooms so I pushed open the door and walked inside.

Three women were lying side-by-side on the bed with their legs in the air. A third was bent over in the gap between the bed and the wall on the far side of the room. Each one was being steadily pounded by a guy. A flash of blonde hair revealed that soccer mom Jenny was among those getting down to it. I was shocked by what I saw. Had I really done this? Maybe it was the fact that I had put the scene behind me, or because I was conscious of the standpoint from which Rob was viewing proceedings, but I began to feel very aware of the strangeness of swinging in a way that I hadn't when I was involved. I went back outside and told Rob that things had got underway.

'I suppose I'd better go and take a look,' Rob said somewhat gravely. After taking a swig from his drink and plonking it on a table, he walked towards the bedroom I had come from. Less than a minute later, he was strolling with exaggerated nonchalance back to the sitting room. 'Everyone seems to be getting on very well in there,' he said with a stunned smile.

We went out onto the apartment's massive balcony, where a handful of party-goers were lounging on the patio furniture, sipping drinks and sharing a joint. In the far corner, meanwhile, Thomas was up to his old tricks. He had positioned a clearly inebriated girl over the hand rail, hitched up her skirt and was working on achieving penetration. Another woman appeared to have taken exception, and was crouching in front of the girl reminding her that she was under no obligation to do anything. I felt ill. I also wanted another vodka. Rob had just lit up a cigarette, so he stayed outside while I went to the kitchen.

What happened next is a bit of a blur. I remember chatting briefly to a guy I had spotted earlier in the night, but I wasn't attracted to him and it was a pretty harmless conversation. I then went into the bathroom, but as I tried to close the door it was suddenly wrenched back open. Before I knew what was happening, there were punches raining down on me. It was the drunken junkie-like girl from earlier. Within ten seconds, some of the guys from the party had dragged her outside kicking and screaming, leaving me standing there with a cut forehead, a busted right hand and the beginnings of a black eye.

Someone must have told Rob what had happened. The girl was still stomping around in the hallway, so he brought me back onto the balcony. He tried to calm me down, but I was in hysterics. One minute everything was fine, and the next I was in a fight with some lunatic twice my size. I couldn't believe it. I was furious with her, and angry with myself for not pulling her eyes out. I had put away a considerable amount of drink that night, which didn't help. At first I had no idea why she would want to attack me, and then I remembered. The guy I spoke to while fixing my drink in the kitchen was the chap she had arrived with. It was a bizarre reason to attack someone, but she was in such a state that it must have made sense in her frazzled head.

Despite the best efforts of Rob and some of the others from the party, I just couldn't calm down. One second I wanted to run out after her, and the next I wanted to hide in a dark corner and cry my eyes out.

After a half an hour of alternating between ranting and sobbing, Rob took me home. We decided the walk might help to clear my head, and it did. 'You've got plenty to write about, anyway,' I said.

By the time we covered the thirty-minute walk to my place, I was starting to feel like myself again. Rob thanked me for helping him out and promised to get in touch once his article was finished. I went inside and curled up on the sofa. My one-night return to the scene had been an utter, utter disaster. At the time, I couldn't have imagined where it would lead.

That night was an eye-opener. Seeing a party up close again after so long, especially one I had gone to without the intention of getting involved in, gave me an opportunity to see the scene in a different light. Even without the drama of the night's end, I just didn't feel like I fitted in in the way that I once did. It was strange, because I had only been away from it all for a few months by then. The night had been fun, especially seeing that room suddenly shift so dramatically from polite conversation to ludicrously wild sex in a matter of minutes, but I had felt like an outsider looking in.

I once would have argued that it was perfectly normal for a girl to take a rational decision to throw herself into the scene, but I was beginning to accept that there were other factors at play. I knew the scene was an extreme and potentially damaging environment, but I had pushed myself into it regardless; and at an unusually young age. That sort of recklessness didn't suggest someone making a rational decision based on the pros and cons. Sure I liked sex, but so do lots of girls, and they wouldn't dream of going to the lengths I had to get it.

After mulling it over, I came to the conclusion that there was probably no one reason why I had been getting in so deep into such an extreme lifestyle. My shyness and largely self-imposed isolation as a kid contributed, as did my exposure to the darker side of the internet and my craving for attention. Throw in drink, boredom, some self-destructive tendencies and a feeling that my life was rudderless and you've pretty much got it. I don't want to sound like a patient stretched out on a psychiatrist's couch ditching all personal responsibility by blaming their parents, but I hadn't exactly had the upbringing of your normal girl next door. If I did, I don't think I would have done the things I did.

I wondered about the motives of the other girls I met through the scene. It was hard to say if they got into it because of some dark issue in their past. I met most of them on just one or two occasions and I didn't delve into the pasts of the ones I did meet more than once; everyone did their best to keep things casual and fun. It was difficult to come to any firm conclusions but from what I knew of the girls I met, I couldn't look at them and say they were all completely normal. Same went for the guys.

Any type of out-of-the-ordinary bedroom antics were so taboo, especially in Ireland, that I felt like there had to be something unusual about someone's psyche, or at least their outlook, to prompt them to go digging around in a place like the scene. I think we all had to be a bit nuts.

Rob's article went live on Joe.ie a few days later. He called me when it was posted on the website and I scrambled onto the net to read it the first chance I got. It gave a full account of how we had met, how we put together our plans and how the night itself had gone down. I never thought that I would be interesting enough to warrant an article, but Rob's piece changed my mind. It was a really interesting read.

I had naturally assumed that the article would be both the beginning and the end of my involvement with the media, but as it turned out it was just the start. Rob called later that day to tell me that his office had been bombarded with calls from producers from radio stations around Ireland. They had read the article. They wanted to bring the two of us on air to talk about it.

I couldn't get over the level of interest the piece triggered. I had agreed to help Rob out with the article because I thought it would be a bit of fun to sneak around doing a cloak-and-dagger investigation into swinging, but I never could have imagined it would take off in the way it did. I mean, I had always assumed that there were a lot of people out there who had a sneaky interest in the scene but would never be willing to actually dip their toes in. I suppose the media just had a nose for what the public wanted.

Over the next few days, Rob and I appeared on a string of radio stations. The live-on-air interviews would start with Rob revealing his alarm at what he found at the party before I would be brought into the conversation. I was quizzed about my sex life, my motivation, my childhood and basically every other aspect of my life I would normally never consider discussing with anyone. The interviewers attempted to probe as deeply as they could to see if I had some sort of mental deficiency or profound emotional damage propelling me into what they saw as a destructive way of living. Occasionally, the host would refer to the shocked and alarmed text messages that poured in from morally outraged members of the public.

It could be pretty nerve-wracking walking into radio studios or waiting on a phone line to be introduced by a show presenter and then brought into a conversation about something so personal. But once I had the first couple of interviews under my belt I started to get used to it. Then I started to enjoy it.

Despite being quite secretive over the years about what I did I had no major problem talking about my past in this context. My name had been changed and nobody knew who I was, so I wasn't risking much. In any case, most of the important people in my life already knew enough about me for my involvement not to come as any kind of surprise.

Some of the interviewers would do their best to roll out the hard questions, but most of them were pretty nice guys and they would generally wind up joking with Rob and I while the horrified text messages from a scandalised general public came in waves.

It was a fun way to round off what was starting to look like the end of my time involved in Ireland's underground sex scene. By then, I was wondering what direction to go in. I felt ready to find someone. I had been involved in swinging for over a year and a half and I wanted to go on dates and be normal. But rather than feeling like a damaged, brutalised refugee from my old life, I was feeling good about myself. I had gone into the scene self-conscious and shy, but the experience had brought me out of my shell. It had made me feel attractive and wanted for the first time in my life. I felt looked after. Knowing that people found me attractive boosted my confidence and helped me realise there was nothing to justify the things I felt about myself as a teenager. I now found it easy to mix with people, and I was soon building a circle of friends that knew little or nothing of my old life. The awkward wall flower was gone.

In fact, I was so comfortable around men that I was becoming a man-eater. I had no problem walking right up to a guy and telling him I thought he was hot. Months of being bombarded with compliments and being surrounded by people who would bend over backwards to be with me had left me with bags of self-assurance. I knew of course that it wasn't exactly the same as being complimented by the people I walked past on the street, but the net effect was the same. It still worked.

But my old ways did manage to come back to haunt me. A few weeks after my last party, I was introduced to a guy by a girl I worked with who was concerned about my long-held singleton status. He had nothing to do with my online life and didn't know anything of my time as a swinger. We were getting on well until, half way through our first date, he told me that he recognised me. He had seen me stripping online. It was Marcus all over again.

As it turned out, he wasn't that bothered. In fact, he was turned on by the whole thing and I ended up going back to his place that night. We had a good time, but I knew it was unlikely that a relationship would develop from it. This worried me. Even when I tried to go straight, when I went on a normal date with a guy I met through normal channels, my old life followed me.

I had been on a handful of pretty dull dates when I decided to meet up with Kevin. We first got in touch on a normal, non-sex-orientated dating website, but I was reluctant to meet up with him. He had a shaved head in his profile photo and it made him look like a bit of a lunatic. Doc Martins and a bomber jacket completed his odd, punk-ish look. He wasn't at all what I would normally go for.

Kevin seemed nice, though, and after chatting on MSN I found we actually had a lot in common. I asked him if he had any other pictures and when he sent me some, I was instantly delighted I had persevered. With his hair grown out and when he was wearing slightly less alarming clothes, the guy was drop dead gorgeous. He was mixed-race and had dark hair and intense green eyes, and he was clearly no stranger to a gym. We discovered that we went to some of the same pubs around Dublin so rather than arranging a one-on-one date, we decided to steer our respective groups of friends to a bar called the Woolshed. Kevin and his friends arrived after we did, and I spotted him as soon as he came through the door. He was even better looking in person, so I decided there was absolutely no point in hanging around. I gulped down my drink and walked right up to him and his friends and said, 'So where's that drink you said you'd buy me?'

We hit it off and went home together that night. We saw each other the following day, and the day after that. Then we were spending all our free time together. Right from the beginning, it felt comfortable. We had a lot of fun together and it just felt right.

Kevin and I were lying in bed together one day, after we had been seeing each other for about a month, when out of nowhere he turned and looked at me. 'I love you,' he said, before quickly turning away again.

The poor guy had been petrified to tell me how he felt in case I didn't tell him I felt the same. He told me later he felt a bit stupid saying it so early on, when we had only been together for four weeks, but he said those were his genuine feelings at the time. I understood how he felt. It's a cliché, but it really felt like we had known each other for years. In any case, he had nothing to worry about. I was in love with him too.

I decided from the off that I wouldn't hide anything from Kevin and although he was reluctant to hear the gory details, my past wasn't an issue for him. I thought at first that this meant my old life would stay firmly where it was but, inevitability, it did creep up on me again.

We couldn't keep our hands off each other when we first got together but for a long time it was just sex. I didn't expect to seamlessly transition from meaningless romps to romantic love-making right from the off, but I was still disappointed. We had a lot of sex, and it was great, but it was the same detached, unemotional fucking I had when I was seeing guys through the scene. And worse was to come. After a couple of months the heat seemed to disappear from the relationship and we started taking to the bedroom less and less. It dropped off to once a week and then to once a fortnight. I was losing the enthusiasm for sex I once had. After a lot of introspection, I realised why. I knew Kevin loved me and I felt I didn't need to have sex with him all the time to keep him. It was selfish in some ways, but it also revealed the level of comfort I felt with him, and it said something quite profound about my attitude towards sex. It took time, but Kevin and I worked at it, and our sex life eventually stopped being just mechanical fucking. Neither was it a tool I used to get him to love me. It felt like something far deeper.

I could count on the fingers of one hand the number of days we spent apart from each other during our first year together. We would go to the gym together, play computer games and although I drank a fraction of what I once did, we would go out and socialise together too. We didn't quite become one of those lovey-dovey romantic couples, but I felt like I had found the person I had been looking for. I think he felt the same way, too.

We moved in together after a few of months. We got a small apartment close to the centre of the city. Rental apartments don't come cheap in central Dublin so we decided to get a place along with one of Kevin's friends, an American guy called Leroy. He and Kevin had been living together when we met and he seemed really cool.

With a new apartment and a new relationship, everything felt like it was falling into place for me. Even my work life started going well. I applied for a job as manager of a retail outlet in one of Dublin's main shopping centres and despite feeling like I was grossly under-qualified for it, I got a phone call the day after my interview to say I had got it. It was far more responsibility than I'd ever had in a job, but I loved it. Work had always been something to be endured rather than enjoyed and I tended to coast through with as little effort as possible. It wasn't that I was lazy, but I found it difficult to motivate myself to be gung-ho about the idea of handing half my life over to the process of making someone else money in exchange for a few euro. My outlook changed in my new role. It was a small company and they had trusted me to run one of their key stores. I stopped feeling like a put-upon wage slave being drained of every ounce of value by some remote corporation who didn't give a shit about me. If I did well in my new job then so did the company. And if the company did well then so did I. I felt like I had become part of a team.

One of the side-effects of my new position was that I was in a main thoroughfare of a major city centre shopping centre for most of my day. Inevitably, I started to spot people I had met from the S&M and swingers' parties. It wasn't that I was embarrassed about what I'd done, but I didn't want the people I worked with finding out either. It wasn't the type of thing I wanted to chat about in the canteen during breaks.

I remember one day, when I had been working there for a month or two, I spotted a guy I recognised. I had met him online on a swingers' website. We got on well and I was attracted to him, so we arranged to be at the same party that weekend. Then we fucked each other's brains out. He was walking towards me as I was going into my shop when I caught a glimpse of his face. I felt a sudden ripple of terror. I had visions of him running towards me with his finger pointed, screaming, 'I know what you did! She's a whore!' Instead, he just looked the other way. I'm not sure he even recognised me, but I was gone before he had the chance to get a second look.

I also ran into Peter – the guy who brought me to that first eye-opening party. He turned up in my shop one day. He told me he had finished with it all and that he now had a girlfriend. He asked if I was still involved, but I told him I had stopped too. We smiled at each other and he went on his way. He had to collect his girlfriend's brother, he said. He had gone back to living a normal life. I wondered if I had really managed to do the same.

As my relationship with Kevin developed, my old life started to feel like it had happened a million years ago. Within months it was feeling like another lifetime. I hadn't become intolerant of the scene, but being with Kevin made it impossible for me to even consider going to a party. I wouldn't have been able to be with another guy now that I was attached and the sight of Kevin with another girl would have killed me. It might make me a hypocrite given the number of boyfriends and husbands I'd been with while their partners were in the same room, but I don't think I would have been able to fight down the urge to punch any girl who laid a finger on him squarely in the face. Knowing what being in a proper, live-in, grown-up relationship was like made it difficult for me to understand how partners could hand each other over in that way.

But I had to admit, sometimes I did miss the scene. I missed the social side, and I missed not knowing how my night would end up. I missed the anticipation, the getting dressed up, the excitement. Strangely, what I didn't miss so much was the sex with different people. I enjoyed being with one person.

In the end, I started to lose touch with the people I had met through the scene. One by one, they disappeared from my life. Either that or I disappeared from theirs. Angelina and I had got really close but in the end, we went our separate ways too. When I first decided to move away from the scene and I decided that the crazy drinking had to go too, I wanted to keep myself busy with other things. I wanted to take the focus off going out, getting pissed and fucking around. I started going to the gym regularly and even found an alternative adrenaline source by taking up martial arts classes. Angelina didn't understand that, and she felt like I was ditching her. She wasn't the type of friend you could go without seeing for months and then hang out with like you had never been apart. She could be quite demanding as a friend. She used to call me every day or two, and then keep me on the phone for hours at a time. Between work, training and Kevin, I just didn't have the hours to spend on over-long phone calls.

In the end, Angelina decided to call a halt to our relationship. She sent me an e-mail explaining, basically, that she didn't want to be my friend any more. She said I wasn't staying in contact enough. It felt like she was breaking up with me.

What I do know is that Angelina stopped swinging shortly after I did. She got into a relationship with someone she met through work and from what I hear they're still going strong. Her new boyfriend even added me on Facebook. I found that strange because I'm also Facebook friends with Angelina's sister and with her daughter, but not with Angelina herself.

Chapter Sixteen

Kevin and I had been together for about a year when suddenly, out of nowhere, he started acting like a complete dickhead. He started to criticise me constantly and everything I did suddenly became wrong. We didn't argue about anything big and there was no major event or catastrophe, but little things became a problem for him. He complained about the way I cleaned. If I made dinner for us he would nit-pick about the way I had cooked it. If we went to the gym together and he didn't like the way I was doing some aspect of my workout, he would warn me that I was going to get fat.

I couldn't figure out the reason behind the sudden change. It seemed like the harder I tried to keep him happy, the more of a critical arsehole he became. It was upsetting. It got to the stage where it felt almost like he was bullying me. Worse, our housemate Leroy seemed to have turned against me as well and he would often join in with Kevin. It was like the two of them were ganging up on me.

Out of nowhere, it was like Kevin just stopped giving a shit. He stopped caring about me completely. I remember one night when I was upset at something stupid he had said to me, I told him I was going to go to bed early.

'Great,' he said. 'Me and Leroy will get a bit of peace.'

He didn't care that I was upset. He didn't even ask if I was okay. He and his friend just stayed up playing video games.

After about a month and a half, I told my mam about it. She said it sounded to her like Kevin wanted to break up but that he didn't have the balls to just come out with it. Instead, she thought he was being a deliberately dick so I'd be the one to take the tough decision to break up.

I decided I had to confront Kevin about his shitty behaviour. I asked him flat out if he wanted to be with me. He stood there looking sheepish before telling me that he wasn't sure. It was pathetic. He suddenly looked like a completely different person to me. My mam was right – he had no balls. Even when I was making it easy for him he still couldn't give me a straight answer.

I asked him how long he had felt that way and he said since Christmas – three months earlier. Worse, we had moved into a new place together between Christmas and March while he had been feeling like this.

'That benefits nobody,' I said. 'Why didn't you just tell me?'

After he offered some half-arsed excuse I suggested we give it a week to see if we could sort things out. He started being a little bit nicer to me but it just wasn't enough. It was obvious to both of us that we were coming to the end. After a couple of days I told him that I didn't see any point in us being together. He agreed. So, in the end, he had got his way. I broke up with him so he didn't have to.

I trawled back over my memory of the previous months to try to figure out where we had gone wrong. We had problems in the bedroom early on but it had felt like things in that department had been getting better. But there were other issues. I remembered that around Christmas he had told me that he felt like we were a becoming a boring couple; that we were stuck in a routine. I had gotten quite defensive about it at the time, pointing out that I worked long shifts and that there wasn't much I could do about it. I said that if we were boring then it wasn't just down to me. He was no more interesting than I was.

On reflection, I probably shouldn't have reacted that way but having the 'boring' tag thrown in my direction, even when he was criticising himself with it as much as he was me, really stung. I could have been accused of being a lot of things in my life, but I thought at least that boring could never have been one of them.

Maybe the comment bothered me so much because it had suddenly become alarmingly close to the truth. We had slipped into a routine – and remarkably quickly. Right from when we first met we had been spending almost all of our time together. We lived together, we went to the same gym and we hung out together every day when we weren't working. Maybe it was just too much. We didn't have lives of our own.

Our lives were each other. I think it made the rot set in that bit faster than it may have otherwise.

Anyway, even if I didn't realise it at the time, that 'boring' conversation must have been the beginning of the end for him. Maybe I could have handled it a bit better but I didn't feel bad about it. It just added insult to injury that he had been harbouring these feelings for so long but had decided to keep them to himself.

Unfortunately, as much as the two of us wanted out, a short, clean break proved impossible. We were still living together and I wasn't in a position to move out at the drop of a hat. I had to find another place to live first and then there was the small matter of saving up the deposit I would need to move in.

There was quite clearly no going back and within a couple of weeks, the two of us started looking elsewhere. Kevin started going on dates and I decided to go on one too. I knew that it was pretty likely that one or other of us would get into something physical eventually, but I didn't see any point in rubbing it in each other's noses. We had been together a long time and it seemed a little disrespectful.

'Will you do me one favour?' I asked Kevin one

night before he went out. 'If you do meet someone, maybe don't bring her home while I'm still living here.'

I was relieved when he agreed. For my part, I certainly wouldn't consider doing that to him.

The first couple of weeks after the break-up were surprisingly civil, but then things started going downhill. I viewed a room in a shared house at the other side of the city centre, and loved it. I agreed to sign on the dotted line and was all set to move in the following week. I told Kevin and Leroy I would be gone in a few days. Then it fell through at the last minute – and Kevin got extremely frosty. We had a row and he said that it looked to him like I didn't want to move out. He had somehow got it into his head that I wanted to stay there so that I could ruin the fun he and Leroy would otherwise be having. It was ridiculous. My world had very much stopped revolving around Kevin and I had absolutely no desire to be there. Moving can take time. That was the extent of it.

The two of them went out that weekend. I had work the next day so I had an early night. Then I woke up at

4 a.m. to the sound of them coming in – and to a woman's voice. I thought, fair play to Leroy, he's scored some girl. But then I heard Leroy saying, 'Good night you two,' and the sound of his door closing. I knew exactly what it meant. Kevin had brought a girl home.

I decided right away that although we had broken up, there was no way I was going to lie in the room next to his listening to the two of them having sex. I had no interest in being with Kevin again but I was stunned that he would be so disrespectful towards me. He had given me his word that he wasn't going to do this. I wasn't going to take it. The shit was going to hit the fan.

I jumped out of bed, got dressed and went to the sitting room. Leroy was still awake, lying on the sofa. I asked him why he wasn't in the room he and Kevin shared. He told me that he decided to let Kevin have it while he crashed out on the sofa.

'I'm not stupid, Leroy,' I said, pushing down my anger as best I could. 'Did Kevin bring a girl home?'

Leroy's face blushed. He didn't know where to look. 'Well you've been seeing other people too!' he blurted.

It was true. I had been on one date, but I didn't sleep with the guy and I certainly didn't bring him home to the place I still shared with my ex.

'But I didn't bring anyone here,' I said. 'I went out on one date with a guy and that was it.'

I got upset. I didn't want to, but I just couldn't believe Kevin would act that way. I had tried really hard to keep a cool head throughout the break-up and to keep things as civil as I could. I wanted the split to be as painless as possible and I didn't try to fight against what Kevin had wanted. But this was like a kick in the teeth. Even if Kevin had decided that he didn't give a shit about me any more, I thought he would at least keep to his word.

Then the girl Kevin brought home came out of the bedroom. In fairness to her, she looked distraught. She said she was sorry for coming back and told me that the only reason she had was because Kevin had told her that I had already moved out. Reading between the lines, it meant they had been seeing each other for a while. This guy just got better and better. I wasn't angry with her. She hadn't done anything wrong, so I didn't see the point in giving her a hard time about it. She went back to the room, grabbed her stuff and then left. After the door slammed shut behind her, I went into Kevin's room.

'What the fuck are you doing?' I asked Kevin, who was lying on his bed in his boxers.

He gave some incomprehensible slur by way of an answer. He was hammered.

'Well, your new girl is gone now, I'm guessing she's pretty pissed off with you and you've also lost any respect I had for you. So well done.'

With that, he leapt out of bed and punched a wardrobe, breaking the door and injuring his hand.

'Okay great,' I said, wondering how much more ridiculous this man could get. 'You're a complete dickhead.'

I was in work the following day when Kevin texted me saying that we needed to talk. I asked if it was going to be just me and him, or if Leroy was going to be there to help him out. He said it would be just the two of us, so I agreed to talk to him back at our place that evening.

'How's your head?' I asked, not really giving a shit either way.

'Terrible,' said Kevin. He then went into a lengthy, self-pitying monologue about how bad his hangover was and how he had a really sore hand from punching a wardrobe. He then told me that he had decided to go after the girl he had brought home that night. Problem was, she lived about twenty kilometres away and he had to get a taxi. When he arrived, she wouldn't answer the door to him so he had to get a taxi back.

'It cost me €80!' he said incredulously.

When Kevin was finished with hard hard-done-by tale, he apologised for bringing her home. He had always been stubborn so I appreciated that he would accept responsibility without me asking him to. But it wasn't much of a consolation. I told him that the fact that he had said sorry showed that he obviously regretted it and had not meant to do it. But it hadn't undone anything. He had still done it and it had showed me what type of character he had.

Strange as it sounds, the way he had acted soon began to look like a good thing. It made me feel better about the fact that we had broken up. I got to see what he was really like. I wasn't missing anything by not being with him.

But one thing was certain – I had to get out of the apartment urgently. I had come to be quite close with Leroy's ex-girlfriend and one night, while we were bonding over a mutual hatred of our ex-boyfriends, she told me I could crash on her sofa for a while. So, I moved my stuff to my dad's place, packed a week's worth of clothes and took her up on her offer. After a week of crashing on her sofa, I found a place sharing with two friendly male singletons. Leroy's ex had been cool about it, but I felt like a total bum sleeping on her couch. It was a low-point in my life I was glad to put behind me.

Kevin and I would still occasionally see each other in the gym, and we managed to stay civil. He met another girl had quickly slipped into a relationship with her. However, there was one last bout of Kevin-related drama to come. A couple of months after I'd moved out, somebody posted a message on a dating website saying, 'Call this number for a good time.' Whoever it was had included Kevin's mobile number underneath. He came to the conclusion that it must have been something to do with me. He called me and said he had thought that maybe Leroy's ex and I might have got drunk together some night and then decided to put it up for a laugh.

'People have been sending me pictures of their dicks,' said Kevin grimly.

When I stopped laughing, I felt pretty insulted. 'Do you think I just sit around thinking about you all the time? It's been months since we broke up. I've better things to do with my time.'

Hilarious as it was to picture Kevin being bombarded with knobs of various shapes and sizes, his new girlfriend didn't see the funny side. She logged into Kevin's Facebook and deleted me from his friends list and then blocked me. It was pretty childish stuff and it said a lot about Kevin's new relationship. Anyway, the whole thing had got boring. I just didn't care any more and I was glad it was finally, firmly, permanently over.

Beyond that first, fairly uneventful first date I went on shortly after Kevin and I had broken up, not much happened in my love life for quite a while. I was too busy trying to avoid homelessness. Once I settled into my new place and put Kevin behind me, it was time to start thinking about what was going to come next. I didn't want to plunge right back into the swinging scene, but I didn't see the harm in checking out some dating websites. Before long, date offers were rolling in and I was soon seeing a couple of guys a week. The way things had gone with Kevin left me feeling like I just wasn't ready to get back into a serious relationship. I didn't see the point in putting myself in a position where I would be hurt. I needed to take some time out so I decided to concentrate on having fun. I wanted to go on dates and instead of hoping for a relationship, to focus on having a good time and seeing where it went.

My gradual return to internet dating was kicked up a gear when I badly hurt my ankle coming down the stairs. It swelled up like a balloon and the doctor told me that while I hadn't broken anything, it was a pretty severe sprain. As a result, I would be pretty much housebound while it repaired itself.

I couldn't work. I couldn't got to the gym. And boredom kicked in. I decided to go back onto a swingers' website to check out who was or wasn't still involved. Just out of interest, of course. I recognised some profiles so I thought, what's the harm in logging back on to chat with them? Before I knew it, I was back on webcam. Just like it always had, things started off with normal conversations before, inevitably, it developed into something more. I was heading down a familiar path.

I arranged to meet a guy from the site who I liked the look of. He was dark-haired, dark-eyed and had a body to die for so when he suggested getting a hotel room I didn't take much convincing. I met another guy a few days later and the following week, I met five guys five days in a row. The normal life I was leading had suddenly disappeared and I was now careening headlong back into an endless cycle of gangbangs and gimp suits. To make things worse, the sex wasn't as enjoyable has it had been. I don't know whether it was me or them, but it was all a bit of a let-down. It made me take a step back and ask myself what the fuck I was doing. Was this really what I wanted? Was I going to fall back into this lifestyle every time I got bored?

In the end, I decided that enough was enough. It just wasn't for me any more. I deleted my profile from the swingers' website and shut my laptop. I would be sticking to normal dating from now on. If I was attracted to a guy and it went well, then sleeping with him might be on the agenda. If we got on really well then I was open to the idea of it becoming something more serious. I began to see the ridiculousness of deciding what I wanted to get from a guy before I'd even gone on a date with him. I could be binning what could develop into a fantastic relationship with someone because I'd decided that week that all I needed from life was casual sex. Equally, going on the hunt for a relationship and a relationship only just heaped on the pressure and stripped any fun out of the getting-to-know-each other process. Anyway, I think guys can smell that on you.

Chapter Seventeen

Noel is tall, broad, shaven-headed and has tribal tattoos down his arms. He has a nasty-looking scar on his face too, but he's so rough-cut gorgeous that it really works. He's exactly the type of guy that has always made me stop and stare on the street.

We first met on a dating website, chatted all week and then arranged to go on a date that weekend. We went for dinner in the Hard Rock Café in Dublin's Temple Bar and hit it off straight away. He gave me a lift back to my place and I asked him if he wanted to come in. We had a cup of coffee before migrating to my bedroom.

While we were having sex, he put his hands around my throat. 'How does it feel?' he asked.

'I like it,' I mouthed silently.

The he tightened his grip. I didn't tell him to

stop, so he went tighter again. It felt amazing. I had heard asphyxiation could amplify orgasms – and it's true. I came so hard I nearly blew the top of my head off.

The surprising turn of events made for some interesting pillow talk that night. I told him I liked being dominated. I added that when dealing with a big guy, it was even more attractive. He told me that that was role he liked to assume anyway. It wasn't the first time I'd heard that.

Interestingly, I hadn't done or said anything to give away what I preferred in the bedroom before that night. Neither had he. It made me wonder how I managed to keep attracting guys who were into being dominant. And how they managed to keep finding me. I mentioned to a male friend of mine what I had been getting up to with Noel and he told me that he loved doing the same thing. Maybe most guys are like that. The world might actually be filled with millions of budding Christian Greys. Still, I decided to hang onto the one I had, and Noel and I have been seeing each other ever since.

Asphyxiation is a dangerous game, but I feel safe

with Noel. I know he's able to control himself. Doing it with the wrong guy – if he isn't able to control himself or he goes too far – could leave you badly hurt or even in the ground.

Noel and I don't see each other as often as Kevin and I did and I like it that way. It has made me realise that I enjoy my own space. I like my own company. I never say never, but I really don't know if I would want an all-consuming 24/7 relationship like that again. I'm certainly not actively seeking one either with Noel or elsewhere. I just have no interest living my life so tightly wound in with someone else's.

Do I regret my time on the scene? The webcams, the swinging, the fetish parties. No. I'm glad I got involved. It happened at the perfect time for me. I was young, I was single and I was bored. In fact, I think I would be regretting it now if I had chosen not to go for it. I met a lot of interesting people and saw things most normal Joe Soaps will live and die without ever getting a glimpse of. It was an experience.

As time has passed, my recollections of that time

have begun to seem alien. Looking back I'm amazed I managed to go through with it all. Getting my story down on paper has brought back a lot of memories of things I did but had almost completely forgotten about. It has dragged up a lot of baggage, but it has also helped put it all more firmly behind me.

Would I recommend getting involved in the scene? It's hard to say. It can be fun and it can be exciting. I'm glad I did it, but switching off my emotions for so long had a knock-on effect that did make things difficult during the early days of my relationship with Kevin. It felt like it might have left a mark I wouldn't be able to erase but, we managed to get past that. We may have gone our separate ways but I don't think my past played a part. I feel I can safely say I've been able to walk away unscathed. In fact, it's been an empowering experience.

There are things I've discovered about myself that I'll take with me. I'm a submissive and I think I always will be. When I was a shy thirteen-year-old girl hanging around internet chatrooms in the hope of finding some company, this made me vulnerable and, looking back, I'm lucky I didn't get seriously hurt. Yahoo Chat in particular was a nest of vipers in those days and it's good that it has been shut down. Risks still exist, but kids are afforded more protection online than they were in the early days of internet for the masses. It's more difficult for predatory men to get in contact with young girls in the anonymous way they once could.

The men I met at fourteen or fifteen took advantage of my naivety, my age and my shyness but I've always had a drive to experiment. As I got older I became more confident in how I dealt with the men I met online and through the scene I stopped being a victim. At the swingers' parties and fetish clubs there was always a line – that I wouldn't do anything whatsoever I wasn't comfortable with – and it was never, ever crossed. Today, my relationship with Noel is about two equals; it's just that in the bedroom (or on the sofa, or in the kitchen) I've given him my permission to take the lead. This dynamic keeps our relationship deliciously exciting.

A big, tattooed handsome bastard who enjoys pulling my hair and choking me while we fuck isn't exactly a traditional storybook ending, but it works for me. I don't know where the relationship will go but even if it ends tomorrow, I know I'll be okay. My happiness isn't pinned to it. I haven't ridden off into the sunset with a knight in shining armour, but I've found my own happy ending.

Acknowledgements

Katie Collins

A big thanks to the guys at Y Books for their fantastic work on our project, and to Rob for creating a book from what would have otherwise been an unknown part of my life. Biggest thanks go to my mam for always accepting me for who I am and encouraging me to be myself.

Robert Carry

This book is for my da. This would've made him smile.

Thanks to Emma, Louise and Nick for saying enough nice things about my early drafts to convince me to stick with it. Also, huge thanks to Karina for her patience in dealing with my blanket refusal to speak about any subject other than this book for whole weeks at a time. A big thank you to the good people at Y Books for giving me my first published title, and to Turlough for helping me out when I was a starving student hoping to someday make a living through writing. Also, thanks to Katie for taking a punt on an unproven writer in the face of bigger and better offers. Hope you like it. A final thanks to my mammy for being thoroughly convinced, even in the face of mounting evidence to the contrary, that it would all be grand in the end.

*Prefer to keep your fantasies within
the pages of a book?*

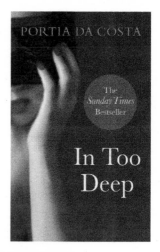

Find out more at www.blacklace.co.uk